Stephenie Meyer

Stephenie Meyer

The Unauthorized Biography of
the Creator of the Twilight Saga

Marc Shapiro

MACMILLAN CHILDREN'S BOOKS

First published in the US 2010 by St. Martin's Press

This edition published in the UK 2010 by Macmillan Children's Books
a division of Macmillan Publishers Limited
20 New Wharf Road, London N1 9RR
Basingstoke and Oxford
Associated companies throughout the world
www.panmacmillan.com

ISBN 978-0-330-51905-2

Copyright © Marc Shapiro 2010

The right of Marc Shapiro to be identified as the
author of this work has been asserted by him in accordance with the
Copyright, Designs and Patents Act 1988.

All rights reserved. No part of this publication may be
reproduced, stored in or introduced into a retrieval system, or
transmitted, in any form or by any means (electronic, mechanical,
photocopying, recording or otherwise), without the prior written
permission of the publisher. Any person who does any unauthorized
act in relation to this publication may be liable to criminal
prosecution and civil claims for damages.

1 3 5 7 9 8 6 4 2

A CIP catalogue record for this book is available from
the British Library.

Printed and bound in the UK by CPI Mackays, Chatham ME5 8TD

This book is sold subject to the condition that it shall not,
by way of trade or otherwise, be lent, resold, hired out,
or otherwise circulated without the publisher's prior consent
in any form of binding or cover other than that in which
it is published and without a similar condition including this
condition being imposed on the subsequent purchaser.

This book is dedicated to

My wife, Nancy, for her love and support. My daughter, Rachael, who still thinks her dad is pretty hip. My agent, Lori Perkins, for the blood, sweat, and tears. Marc Resnick at St. Martin's Press for the gig. Patrick Jankiewicz, the biggest kid on the block. Elizabeth at Ralphs for the good cheer. Carolina Karimi, who is the future. Chaos: RIP. All the ghosts of loving pets past. John and Linda in the great Pacific Northwest. Mike Kirby, who knows the score. All the great books, all the cool music. And finally this book is dedicated to the vampire in all of us. Bring on the night.

Contents

introduction

Romance Anyone?

The word is romance.

Look it up in the dictionary if you've forgotten what it means. And when you get the clinical meaning, go to the masters of the form.

Romeo and Juliet is a good example, an enduring one if you will. It has all the shudders, the thrills of love at its most chaste and yet most emotional. And for its time and forever more, it has all the angst and tragedy that anybody could ask for. *Wuthering Heights*, which is currently experiencing a resurgence in popularity, is another good emotional exercise. Even *Gone with the Wind*, amid the scope and adventure of the Civil War, is a love story at its core.

The titles are different. The stories remain quite divergent. But there is a reason these books remain uniformly powerful and timeless. It's the love.

Now many years up the line is Stephenie Meyer, who has taken romance to a very different place. A place of the night. A place of supernatural thrills. But, at the end of the day, it's always about the romance, those first feelings and the beating of the heart at the sight of another.

The moment when you know that you will be together forever.

Make no mistake. Stephenie Meyer is not about the physical expression of those feelings that, for better or worse, we have become all too familiar with. You know what we're talking about here. There's no need to spell it out.

You can get that anywhere, figuratively and literally. Any commercial can give you that warm, desirous feeling. Your breakfast cereal can give you that sense of arousal. Movies and television? What can you say? The obvious is the new foreplay. Sadly, courtship, to a very large extent, has gone out the window.

Except in the world of Bella the human and Edward the vampire as chronicled in the books *Twilight*, *New Moon*, *Eclipse*, and *Breaking Dawn*. There it is, the gentle touch, the longing look, the warm embrace, the hand-in-hand walks in the fog-shrouded night in the town of Forks. Oh, and yes, the kiss. Make no mistake, there is the tension and that warm and fuzzy feeling when you know it's first love and it's real. Don't remember those emotions? Talk to your parents. They can clue you in.

In Stephenie Meyer's world, it's everything that leads up to sex . . . without the sex. It's the romance, stupid.

And nobody knows that better than Stephenie Meyer.

Stephenie is old school when it comes to affairs of the heart. Old as in the forties and fifties as portrayed on the silver screen. Old as when the logical conclusion to affairs of the heart were left up to the imagination and the heart. When even the hint of a physical rendezvous was usually played out over a film's end credits or a fade to black.

Stephenie was brought up in a world of genteel thoughts and emotions. She was raised Mormon; in and of itself not a defining factor in her approach to creating imaginary canvases. But her religion, coupled with a loving, conservative sense of self that is her template, is very much the fuel that has fired her work. Being a good girl with good values and a freedom to make the best choice is at the root of her works. Not always the hip and cool personality to present, especially in high school where peer pressure reigns supreme. But then for Stephenie, peer pressure has never been part of her approach to life and her work. Being true to herself has.

She writes of the chaste, lyrical emotions of the courtship. That first look across a crowded room. The early, unsure small talk. The smile. The first feelings of attraction. The heat is present but, in her imagination, it is a warm glow rather than a blazing fire that guides her characters through the dance that is first love.

Yes, there are vampires and other fantastic manifestations in her world and the consequences of a human falling in love with a creature of the night cannot be avoided. But even in this extreme kind of relationship, Stephenie draws on innocence and a quite natural coming-of-age as her signposts rather than the carnal elements that have populated much of the vampire genre in such classics as Anne Rice's *Interview with the Vampire*, Bram Stoker's *Dracula*, and countless other movies and books.

In her books, the vampires are much more civilized, mature, and have a definite moral compass. They drink blood, but it is animal not human, although they can be tempted. They don't turn into bats. They don't sleep in coffins. But they can have conflicts, desires, and emotions. In Stephenie Meyer's world, the line between human and inhuman is blurred. And that is what makes this dance even more enticing.

Make no mistake. The millions of readers of Stephenie Meyer's books are not naïve. In the real world most know where this courtship is heading. Many of them have experienced it firsthand.

But that does not mean that the fairy tale, the warm

moments and memories of first love cannot still be a comforting place to go. A place where Stephenie Meyer has chosen to take us.

The sixties brought the world new freedoms. Stephenie Meyer is leading a heartfelt charge back to a simpler, more romantic, and, yes, a more innocent time.

—Marc Shapiro

one

Fame . . . What's Your Name?

Cave Creek, Arizona, is a chamber of commerce dream. It is an artsy, antique kind of town. Big on family, a sense of community, and just far enough away from the hustle and bustle of Phoenix. The surrounding desert landscape does not so much distract as it does complement the town. It is the type of place people come to relax and get away from it all.

In the case of Stephenie Meyer, it was the kind of place to come, raise a family, embrace her faith, and to live a fulfilling, quiet, and relaxing life.

But when Stephenie Meyer returned to her home in Cave Creek in the summer of 2008, it was far from a quiet time.

You could see it on her face. Her eyes would occasionally reflect that thousand-mile stare that comes from not enough sleep. The tight little smile, which had looked so precious when her first book, *Twilight*, came out, was now often showing a hint of being forced. If you caught any of her television interviews or YouTube videos that were making the rounds in support of her new novel, *The Host*, *Twilight* the movie, and all her previous books, you might have caught some hints of resignation as she waited for the questions she knew were coming and mentally readied herself for the by now automatic responses.

And the endless round of reporters were not making the task easy. That the entire story, by 2008, had been told too many times to count did not stop lazy reporters from asking the "dream" question, the "how does it feel to be famous" question, and the "how did you know so much about vampires" question. It was as if everybody was satisfied with the obvious angles on Stephenie's life and not really anxious to discover more. Which is why things that would occasionally slip out during media interviews and book-signing question-and-answers that should have been of interest rarely rated a note on the numerous Twilight and Stephenie Web sites.

To be sure, there were exceptions to the rule. A *Phoenix New Times* article dug deeper than most and so came away with things we did not know. And although it was all primarily surface glitz and gloss, *Entertainment Weekly* managed to pluck a few nuggets of new info out of the basket. But for the most part it was all the same, repeated to the nth degree. It was enough to drive this mild-mannered Mormon wife and mother turned best-selling author to . . . well, go all vampire on them. But Stephenie was the good soldier, perhaps still at a stage when the excitement of it all had not yet been trumped by the tedium, who smiled until it hurt, and did interviews until her mind turned to mush.

And then limped home . . . to do the work that needed to be done.

Looking forward to some quiet time with her husband and three children after coming off a grueling weeks-long promotional tour, Meyer was immediately thrust into a three-day marathon of fine-tuning *Breaking Dawn*, the final novel in her tale of human and vampire love in the isolated town of Forks, Washington. The book was primed for an August 2008 release with advance orders already clocking in at more than three million.

But despite every sign in the universe pointing to the author having made that final leap to stardom, as recently as early 2008, Stephenie was insisting to everybody who asked, including *Vogue*, that what she had accomplished was still small potatoes.

"It's still a small family business," she said. "It's just a little family thing. I couldn't deal with it if I couldn't keep it small."

By the time she sat down with *Breaking Dawn*, Stephenie had already discovered certain realities of the writing life, not the least of which was the time it was taking away from her family. Not that her husband and children were complaining. They had long since discovered the reality of Stephenie's new life and the shorthand that indicated it was time for her to be alone to write.

Twilight had been written for herself. She has said more times than she can count that she never thought anybody would read it. *New Moon* was essentially finished before *Twilight* was even published. But by the time she sat down to write *Eclipse*, there were agents and publishers to consult with, interviews to do in support of her books, and perhaps most important, deadlines that were constantly in evidence that had to be met and were indicative of a career that had taken off like a comet to the tune of millions of copies sold.

Stephenie admittedly enjoyed the notoriety, but on those days when the obligations of bestselling author became too much, she longed for the days when only a few people knew her name.

"I like being normal," she told the *National Post*. "I like being ordinary. I like going home and just being mom and having my little circle of friends. I'm not Stephenie Meyer to them. I'm just Steph."

The rocket to stardom that now left Stephenie occasionally longing for the simple life was not a sudden invasion in her life. Well into the writing of *New Moon* and the earliest stages of *Eclipse*, Stephenie would say during a 2008 question-and-answer session in a Chicago bookstore, that she was still able to hang on to some semblance of normalcy and routine.

"I would get up, get the kids ready, and send them off to school," she recalled. "If I was being good, I would hit the elliptical machine for a half hour. Then I would flip through TiVo and answer my e-mail. Then I would sit down, slip on my headphones, and write until I heard somebody asking me what we were having for dinner."

For better or worse, as she slipped on some music by Muse and Blue October and tuned herself into editing mode, Stephenie's world had gotten a lot bigger.

Normally Stephenie wrote at night when her family was long asleep and the chance for distractions was slim. But with the pressures and demands of the publishing world at hand, she had begun this final lap with *Breaking Dawn* at 6:00 A.M. and, if she was lucky, burned out, or both, would be finishing up around midnight.

Adding to the craziness was the seemingly endless round of media interviews that saw reporters, despite the fact that she had been on every possible outlet on the last tour, from the likes of *Entertainment Weekly* and *USA Today* making the pilgrimage to Cave Creek to ask the probing questions, the questions she had heard so many times before, and to find out, in many cases, what happens when a happily married Mormon woman with three children has a dream.

A dream that has turned into a worldwide literary sensation, the likes of which hasn't caught the world's collective imagination since a young British single mother named Joanne Rowling scribbled those initial notes about a fantasy world and a young boy with glasses named Harry Potter on a long train ride through the British countryside.

The comparison between Stephenie and J. K. Rowling was one of the first labels to stick. Stephenie was amazed and honored at the comparison but also a bit ambivalent.

"There will never be another J. K. Rowling," Meyer told *USA Today* long after she had heard the comparison between Rowling and herself too many times to count. "That really puts a lot of pressure on me. I'm just happy being Stephenie Meyer. That's cool enough for me."

Meyer's laid-back persona was partially born of an endearing shyness that has followed her from birth. The mild-mannered outsider who was never the life of the party. The consensus from those who knew her pre-*Twilight* was that she was adjusting fairly well to the mantle of bestselling author and that not much had changed since her days at Brigham Young University. And on the surface, Stephenie does seem to present the demeanor of "good sport" about it all. But the author conceded in a recent *Paris Match* interview that celebrity takes a bit of getting used to.

"I don't really know how I'm dealing with celebrity," she offered. "I used to live without being recognized. When I am stopped on the road now, I am always shocked."

Despite the pressure of her newfound celebrity and the increased scrutiny, Meyer remains accommodating and delightfully candid and disarming in a sort of straightforward way that springs full-blown from a highly conservative Mormon upbringing. Her homespun candor, evolved as it has since she began doing press in 2005, has been a quiet breath of fresh air in an often overhyped to the point of overkill pop culture landscape.

Meyer has indicated in many interviews that her modest hopes for the first novel, *Twilight*, "were to maybe get $10,000 to pay off the family's minivan." In her wildest dreams, Stephenie Meyer had no idea what the romance of Bella and Edward, a human who falls in chaste love with a vampire, would bring.

Stephenie Meyer appears the unlikeliest of torchbearers for a brand of what is often dismissed as "chick lit" that has captured the imaginations of young girls and middle-aged women alike. She is as un-vampire oriented as a romantic horror novelist could be.

She has an aversion to horror films and racy literature of any kind. It was only in college and her discovery of satellite radio that she discovered the joys of new music such as Blue October, Muse, Linkin Park, and My Chemical Romance, all of which are constantly plugged into the aural background of her working environment and that have driven her writing spurts over the course of her four romantic vampire novels. But while she has opened up to modern music, Jane Austen and the more genteel side of literature has remained a constant influence and companion.

To this day she is an ardent follower of the Book of Mormon, attends the Church of Jesus Christ of Latter-day Saints, and will not work on Sunday in conjunction with her religious beliefs. During the early editing stages of *Twilight*, an editor suggested that she might do well to add a premarital sex scene to the lyrically romantic but sex-free proceedings. Stephenie said no, most likely more for the integrity of the story, but also, it's safe to say, a by-product of her own moral upbringing where "good girls" were a natural way of being. There would be no sex scene.

In the best possible way, Stephenie Meyer is a walking contradiction.

So it seemed that the young mother from the Arizona suburb of Cave Creek had most certainly gone over to the dark side when she wrote *Twilight*, a story ripe with temptation and otherworldly creatures. At least that's the way Meyer remembered the feedback from the Mormon community.

Stephenie acknowledged in an interview with *ABC News Nightline*, not long after *Breaking Dawn* was published, that her books reflect the way she looks at the world...which is pretty much black and white. "Not big black or big white, just little tiny checkers of it. There's always a right and wrong to the situation."

But even with that defense, convincing many was an uphill battle.

"Some Mormons, especially those who know me, are surprised by my choice of topics," she told the Mormon arts and culture Web site at www.motleyvision.org. "'Vampires,' they say, with a critical lilt in their voices. Then they add self-righteously, 'I don't read those kinds of books.' I hasten to explain to them that it's not like that. I put a lot of my basic beliefs into the stories. Free agency and sacrifice are big themes in what I do. But even after I explain all that, I still have family and friends who look at me funny."

Which is the way that Meyer often looks at herself. As she puts the finishing touches on the book that will bring her total of books in print to twenty-eight million, what's happening to her is still a mystery that she is only beginning to wrap her psyche around.

"I don't really see myself as a professional writer," she confessed in a *Vogue* interview. "I still feel like an amateur."

A lot of people have agreed with that assessment.

Many, including the increasingly cranky Stephen King, have dismissed her as a good storyteller, but not a very good writer. Some critics have demeaned her books as plotless, pointless, and populated with characters with no real substance. Some, at the darker end of the critical spectrum, have gotten downright nasty, calling her a housewife with a hobby who had just gotten lucky.

Not that it would be the first time a less-than-stellar writer has found success. The history of popular fiction has often been top-heavy with lesser-quality writers who had managed to captivate an audience. But no matter what one thinks of Stephenie Meyer's skills as a writer, one thing cannot be denied.

Millions of readers can't wait for more.

Those around her concede that Stephenie has done a wonderful high-wire act with it all. She has studiously avoided all the trappings and ego of being a bestselling author. Early on she was thrilled when twenty people showed up for a signing at a local bookstore.

"I kind of miss those days," she reflected in a *Media-Blvd* magazine interview. "Then we would start getting a hundred people and I would freak out and say 'There's a hundred people out there!' Now we're getting thousands and I just have to suck it up and do my job."

She was largely unfazed by the photo shoots and the early press encounters. Even the occasional negative reviews of her early books were like water off a duck's back. To her way of thinking, suddenly being front and center in the public eye was no different than the years she spent as a nondescript wife and mother.

"I think that after thirty years of being the most normal person in the world, it's really hard to become ungrounded," she said when *USA Today* came calling. "When I'm not doing a book tour or press interviews I just tend to forget all about it."

But that was then. By the time Stephenie began writing *Breaking Dawn*, her sense of privacy was slowly giving way to the intrusion of celebrity, a tale that had been told countless times before.

At a recently concluded book tour stop in Salt Lake City, primarily in support of *The Host*, her first foray into slightly more adult, non-vampire fare, more than a thousand girls and women, many wearing Twilight T-shirts and regalia, screamed at the mere presence of the Twilight author. She was a literary rock star and the baggage was not too far behind.

At one point in the Salt Lake City appearance, a shaking young girl approached Stephenie and stammered that she had been ready to kill herself, but that reading the Twilight books had given her a reason to live. Back at Cave Creek, she was now the local celebrity whose house people stopped by just to stand on the sidewalk or the foot of the driveway and stare. Suddenly it was not so easy to go down to the local deli and have a leisurely lunch. And as she explained in an *Entertainment Weekly* interview, celebrity was beginning to have its price.

She related that initially she and her husband thought it would be cute to put family photos on their Web site but, as her celebrity rose, they removed the photos for privacy's sake. Her home address is now unlisted and any fan letters that do arrive are immediately thrown in the trash. Her home phone is, likewise, unlisted, but occasionally a fan will find out her cell phone number and she is often greeted with teenage giggling when she picks up. There is obvious concern, but she managed to couch it all in a bit of humor during the *Entertainment Weekly* interview.

"Numbers are easy to change," she said. "Moving is harder. They'll have to drag me out of this place on a plank. Before I move, I'm going to put up a fence and get some shepherds."

But while she has taken precautions in the wake of celebrity, Stephenie was quick to point out in a www.canmag.com interview that some days being in the eye of the storm can bring up a lot of different emotions.

"It's all a very strange and surreal thing," she explained. "Most mornings I can get up and just not think about it at all. But then I have to go someplace for business and it's like all of a sudden I can't walk through the front door because I might be seen. It's weird. It's strange. And sometimes it can be real hard for me."

However, ultimately Stephenie Meyer marches to her own beat. And going into late 2008, her mental day planner was looking to the future. There was the last-minute promotion for *The Host*, the rush of press for *Breaking Dawn*, and the November 2008 premiere of the movie version of *Twilight*.

Then, quite simply, she was going to disappear. Well, not completely. Stephenie was going to do what all good writers do. Which is to write.

She has long hinted at a book called *Midnight Sun*, which is the telling of *Twilight* from Edward's perspective. She already has the basic outline of two sequels to *The Host* in place. She's been anxious to tackle her notion of an adult murder mystery, a ghost story, and a book about time travel.

Many have speculated that this rush to take her talents in so many different directions is a not too veiled attempt to avoid the "one-trick pony" tag that is currently dogging J. K. Rowling. Stephenie insisted that was not the case in a conversation with *USA Today*.

"I'm just going to stay home next year and write five books. It may not happen, but that's my goal. It's just going to be about sitting home and writing."

two

Head in a Book

Stephenie Meyer is very much a child of television. In fact, despite a rather highbrow and progressive attitude toward music and literature, it would not be out of the question to describe her as a connoisseur of mainstream television.

She'll drop everything for a *Law & Order* marathon and, these days, bemoans the fact that her heavy workload has caused her to lose touch with favorite reality shows like *Survivor* and *The Amazing Race*. So it comes as no surprise that as a child growing up, she saw herself as living in a television world.

"I always thought of us as *The Brady Bunch*," she reflected in a *Vogue* magazine interview. "We were six children, three boys and three girls. The only thing that was missing was Alice the maid."

Stephenie Morgan was born on December 24, 1973,

in Hartford, Connecticut, the second of what would ultimately turn out to be six children to Stephen and Candy Morgan. The Morgans were cut from traditional stock. They were tradition-bound, very religious, conservative in thought and deed, and valued having a large family.

Being born on Christmas Eve had always resonated with Stephenie in an indifferent way. She never thought of herself as special because of the coincidence of her birthday and has allowed that it is an irony that she would just as soon not make a big deal out of. Her father, a financial planner, always had a streak of whimsy in him and so, when it came to naming his newborn, he opted for the "different" spelling of Stephenie, his first name with an *ie* on the end.

Stephen and Candy Morgan liked the quiet serenity of Hartford and would not have thought twice about staying there forever. But, when Stephenie was four, the reality of a better-paying job for Stephen and more financial security for their ever-expanding brood resulted in the couple relocating to the desert suburb of Glendale, Arizona, in 1977 before relocating to Cave Creek some years later. The growing Morgan clan immediately took to the great outdoors; the children's activities centering around bike riding, the building of playhouses, and, as the boys got older, childhood war games.

"It was a really nice childhood," Stephenie related in

a *CBS Sunday Morning* television interview. "My parents were good parents."

The credo of the Morgan family was that everybody had to pull their own share of the load when it came to household chores and so it fell quite naturally to Stephenie to occasionally play surrogate mom to her younger brothers. She was usually the first on call to babysit them when her parents were busy doing other chores and she became quite adept at changing diapers for her younger siblings. To this day, she often describes those days, again in terms only a true television expert could understand, as fulfilling the "Jan Brady" role in the family hierarchy.

Stephenie was quick to admit during a *Phoenix New Times* interview that her mothering instincts were very much present even as a child. "I used to have mom nightmares about my brothers; when you think about terrible things happening to your kids and you can't stop them. I had those kinds of nightmares about my brothers."

Much of the Morgan family's life centered around their religion and the local Church of Jesus Christ of Latter-day Saints. They quickly became ingrained in the fabric of the local Mormon community and, by association, so did Stephenie. Through the church she came to know a young boy named Christiaan Meyer. It was never more than small talk and Stephenie, to this day, laughingly recalled that they never had what you would call a real conversation and, in fact, barely said a word to each other.

Given her conservative, heavily religious upbringing, it came as no surprise that young Stephenie was a studious reader of the Book of Mormon. But Stephenie's parents were of a more progressive bent when it came to literature. Stephen, a ravenous reader whose wide-ranging tastes included the classic Terry Brooks fantasy, *The Sword of Shannara*, would regularly indoctrinate his children in the books he liked to read rather than what might be age- or religious-appropriate. From her mother, Candy, Stephenie received a steady dose of Jane Austen and the gentle and lyrical side of the classics. And while her siblings were also book readers, for Stephenie books became a positive obsession that was impossible to break.

"I was the bookworm in the family," she told *Vogue*.

To the extent that by her early elementary school years, it was the rare time when the curly haired young girl was not spotted with her head buried deeply in an open book. She has often explained that she would look for the fattest books she could find. Wednesday was library day at her school and Stephenie was usually the first in line to check out *Anne of Green Gables* or other ambitious reads. Then it was off to her room where she would spend hours at a time immersed in her favorite pastime.

"I always had a feeling that reading was an exciting thing and I loved big, fat books," she recalled in a Sunday *New York Times* interview. "I went from *Gone with the Wind* to *Little Women* to *Pride and Prejudice* because they were the biggest books my parents had and they were stories that were not going to end so fast."

Her passion for the written word continued to be encouraged by her parents, and in particular, her father, who would always read to the children before bedtime.

"My father used to read us some stories at night," she told a *Paris Match* interviewer. "He always stopped reading when the suspense would get real high. But I was so anxious to see what happened next that I would sneak down, get the book, and read ahead."

Stephenie's father was not concerned at all that his daughter was spending so much time alone. "She was kind of in her own little world," Stephen Morgan told the *Arizona Republic.* "If she was in a good book, she was perfectly happy off by herself, enmeshing herself in that world."

And the relationship cemented by father and daughter through books was very evident, recalled Stephenie in an interview with www.sheknows.com in 2008.

"My dad and I, through high school, that's how we

communicated. We shared books. He knew what I was reading and I knew what he was reading. That was what we would talk about. That's what kept us close through the difficult years, when parents are the bad guys."

But while Stephenie was a voracious reader, sometimes reading as many as four books a week, she did not seem inclined, whether through insecurity or disinterest, in letting her own imagination out on paper. However, Stephenie has always insisted that she was a born storyteller and it is known that, on long drives to visit their grandparents in Utah, her parents and siblings would often smile as Stephenie would spin nonsensical yarns to stave off the boredom of a long drive.

"My whole life I told myself stories," she said in a www.entertainment.timesonline.com story. "I just didn't think anyone would want to hear them. I was very insecure."

Stephenie's upbringing was conservative, religious, and, by degrees, controlling in a positive way. Stephenie was not allowed to listen to any music before her parents had listened first and given it their okay. Consequently, as she related in a *Rolling Stone* interview, "We wound up listening to a lot of Lionel Richie and Chicago." Her parents were big on church-related activities for their children and easily guided them away from teenage temptations. But rather than serving to drive their children to rebellion—a common perception—it brought the Morgan brood, especially Stephenie, a quiet sense of self.

"Being a good girl came quite naturally for us," she recalled. "So did being a good boy. I don't believe any of us ever associated with what would be considered a bad kid."

Stephenie entered Chaparral High School in 1989. And it is during those years that the young girl appeared to take on the persona of outsider that she would translate to the character of Bella years later. By all accounts, Stephenie maintained her bookish nature and made good grades. She was reportedly always attentive in class, but rarely one to take the lead in discussions.

The young woman continued to read what she considered the classics, Jane Austen and Shakespeare. But she also found time during her high school years to get in touch with such Mormon literary scions as science-fiction writer Orson Scott Card and Jack Weyland. She was also, by her own estimation in a *Breaking Dawn* tour question-and-answer in New York, "A not too bad a painter in high school. I won a few ribbons."

But Stephenie's seeming reluctance to go into any great detail on her high school years in interviews would lead to speculation that these were not the best of times for her. And that her memories of that time might be tinged with a bit of envy. She admitted as much in a moment of candor with *People* magazine when she said she could identify with the character of Bella "because when I was that age I was not in the popular crowd and I was kind of clumsy."

However she did recall in a *School Library Journal* interview that she did experience one very serious crush during her teen years. She has never gone into detail and has never named the boy. All she would say was, "I did fall for somebody once as a teen and it wasn't one of those happy things."

She made no bones about her feelings toward many of her classmates in a bio she offered to the Web site www.yabookscentral.com when she said, "Chaparral was the kind of place where every fall a few girls would come back to school with new noses and there were always Porsches in the student parking lot."

Stephenie also dropped hints that her high school years may have been less than happy times when, in a story that appeared on the Web site FirstStep.me, she advised readers contemplating higher education to "Definitely go to college. High school is miserable. College is where you find out who you really are."

She is also candid in stating that there was the constant presence of premarital sex and other temptations during those formative years in high school and, yes, at Brigham Young University, despite the religious dictums that emphasized celibacy and honor among students.

"A lot of my high school and college experience was about restraint," she told www.entertainment.timeson line.com.

Although her personal life during her high school years has been kept largely private, it is known that she did have some level of a social life, although, as she explained in an interview with RTÉ Entertainment on www.rte.ie.com, it was rather unexceptional.

"My own experiences as a teenager, with dating and stuff, was pretty mundane and unexciting."

One seemingly positive milestone that marked her high school years, and that was chronicled in a London *Daily Telegraph* story, was that in her sophomore year at Chaparral, she held hands with a boy for the first time.

Stephenie graduated from Chaparral High School in 1992. She was glad to finally be escaping the confines of the seemingly shallow, by her standards, environment and, armed with a National Merit Scholarship, she was looking forward to expanding her horizons at Brigham Young University, the educational touchstone for Mormons and a place she felt she could truly be herself.

Brigham Young marked the first real freedom for Stephenie. She was living out of state and in a dorm situation with people she did not know. But she was anxious to get on with this next stage of her life.

She did not have to think too hard about a major.

"I chose to major in English," she told *Phoenix New*

Times. "I don't know if I ever considered anything else. I love reading and this was a major I could read in."

But she would often admit in later years that a big reason for her choice was the continuing fear of taking her creative tendencies to that next step. She figured she could slide through the curriculum on the strength of her papers on classical authors. Anything beyond that and she feared letting people get too deeply into her head.

"Writing about Jane Austen was safe," she told *Vogue.* "It's not like people were going to get inside my head and want to know if I was crazy."

three

Life Goes On

When Stephenie stepped onto the campus of Brigham Young University to begin the fall 1993 semester she had a plan. Unfortunately it was not a plan that inspired too much in the way of confidence.

Because, quite candidly, Stephenie did not, like so many students entering higher education, really know what she wanted to do with her life.

"I figured I would go on [after graduation] and go to law school," she told *Phoenix New Times.* "I wasn't super-concerned with supporting myself because I wasn't thinking much beyond being a student."

Stephenie proved to be quite diligent during her first two years at Brigham Young. She maintained good grades, exercised her creative muscles with painting classes, and basically just floated through academia with her ambition level and any rock-hard plans for the future on hold.

Easily the highlight of her early years at Brigham Young was the opening up of her worldview. Although she was primarily around like-minded people in terms of their religious upbringing, she was slowly but surely discovering a more youthful, progressive bent among her fellow students. She was learning that even fellow Mormons could have different attitudes about politics, culture, and just about everything else. Including, as it turned out, music.

After years of basically having her musical tastes closely monitored and shaped by her parents, Stephenie discovered the joys of satellite radio, which brought the enticing sounds of new music into her world. And Stephenie was particularly entranced by the sounds of nineties rock and all its progressive offshoots. There was something in the lyrics, the rhythms, and the overall vibe of what she was hearing that was taking her to another place.

She was still a babe in the woods when it came to R-rated movies and she was her own censor when it came to books that might contain material of a sexual or violent nature. Although she would admit, some years later, that she did read a couple of Anne Rice's novels during her college years. Stephenie was spreading her wings, but few in her immediate circle had picked up on it.

Despite her constant adherence to her conservative beliefs, Stephenie was inwardly proud and more than a little bit excited to be taking baby steps.

And those baby steps did not just extend to music and books. It is known that Stephenie did date throughout most of her college years, but it was thought that it was simple socializing with nothing serious going on. However, in a 2008 question-and-answer session at a Pasadena, California, book signing, the question of how her own romantic relationships might be influencing her fictional romantic story lines brought a surprising revelation from Stephenie that would lead one to think her college relationships might have been more serious.

"I did go through a long phase of kind of getting engaged a lot," she told the crowd. "I was trying on a lot of different ideas of love."

Stephenie returned home during a break before her senior year at Brigham Young and reconnected with her old church buddy, Christiaan (who, thanks to his grandmother, was pretty much known to everybody as "Pancho"). Christiaan had just recently returned from a Latter-day Saints mission to Chile and appeared much more mature and worldly for the experience. At least initially, Stephenie overlooked those traits. As she said in an interview with the *Phoenix New Times*, her first impression of the now grown Christiaan was "Oh, look who grew up and got cute."

The pair began dating and, as Stephenie jokingly remembered in the same interview, their courtship quickly evolved into a rigid routine. "Our second official date was when he proposed to me for the first time. He would propose to me every night and I would tell him no every night. I think he must have proposed to me over forty times. After a while it just became our end-of-date thing."

Being raised a strict Mormon, Stephenie could kind of understand Christiaan's persistence and, yes, physical urges. Traditionally, relationships develop a lot faster between men and women in the Mormon religion. And the big reason, she reasoned, was the no-sex-before-marriage edict that put pressure on dating couples in some pretty obvious ways.

Stephenie had returned to Brigham Young for her senior year. She remained a committed student, but it became obvious to those around her that she had a lot on her mind. She had grown to love Christiaan very deeply and, because of his persistence, she was coming around to the idea of marriage. There was also the question of what she would do with a degree in English when all she wanted to do was read. And of more immediate importance, there was the one class she needed to take to get her degree that she was dreading.

"I had shied away from creative writing classes throughout my entire college career," she told www.motleyvision.org. "But I had to take one class to get my degree. So I took a class in poetry because I knew I could fake my way through. Even at that point in my life, I was still terrified of creative writing. I didn't think the stories I told myself would be interesting to anyone else and I didn't know if I could produce, creatively, on command."

But on those occasions when she did have to write, she recalled on www.india-forums.com that she would take great pains to mask her creative insecurities. "When I was in college I wrote a paper from the feminist perspective (it's an easy way to write) on *The Princess Bride*."

And which, in the coming years, would prove an intregal perspective that would mark her Twilight series.

Fortunately, what Stephenie found in the college class she dreaded taking was what she has described as an "insanely brilliant" and "fascinating" instructor in Professor Steven Walker. Rather than the chore she was expecting, Stephenie found under Walker's tutelage a heretofore unexpected perspective on literature that allowed her to interpret the books she had been reading for years in a new and different way. She emerged from Walker's class mentally energized to the possibilities of literature.

Walker, in a 2009 interview, recalled that Stephenie

had actually taken two of his classes, Introduction to Literature in the fall 1993 semester and Modern British Literature in the fall 1994 semester, and said, "She was quiet in class, reserved but very much present. The kind of student I like best. I remember that Introduction to Literature was a huge class, with about 110 students. But she stood out among them enough for me to remember her distinctly sixteen years later."

However, while quiet and reserved, Walker was quick to point out that when she had something to say, she said it quite well.

"She talked less than some of the others, but had more to say than most of us when she did speak. She was the kind of student who could energize a classroom conversation with a well-timed comment or provocative question. I always thought she delved more deeply into the literature than many of us and related to it more personally."

Professor Walker recalled that his classes did not require any creative writing, but rather critical assessments of the literature they were reading.

"Those essays could get quite personal," he remembered, "and Stephenie's approach was about as creative as academic writing allows. She was a fine writer who, even at that point, was competing with the best of the eloquent English majors."

Walker recalled three elements that jumped out at

him while reading Stephenie's first critical essays that indicated to him she might have a future as a writer.

"First, she was appealingly honest and personally forthcoming about her genuine reactions. She always made it clear not just where her head was, but where her heart was as well. Second, she had unusually good ideas and fine insights. Stephenie was not just bright, but deeply insightful. Third, she was wonderfully concrete in her style, detailing her ideas through precise and vividly evidenced prose."

Walker is not sure what Stephenie got out of his classes that expanded her horizons. But he did indicate that she was always one to make a lot out of a little.

"I guess the central appeal of our classes to Stephenie was the wide-open possibilities," he said. "Stephenie was superb at what we tried to do, which was to be honest about our personal responses and to stretch our reading horizons of literature. I thought I saw her eyes shine when we talked about things like 'the world is charged with the grandeur of God' in Hopkins's poem or Tennyson's 'Come, my friends, 'tis not too late to seek a newer world.' And I know she was fond of Yeats. The only thing we read together that verged on her current writing venue was Mary Shelley's *Frankenstein*."

Federal law did not allow Professor Walker to divulge what grades Stephenie received in his classes but he did offer, "Stephenie did, as you might imagine, very well."

It was during the later stages of her college years that Stephenie, perhaps inspired by the classes, made her first awkward attempts at getting her creative thoughts down on paper. She remembered writing "some really bad poetry" and writing a handful of short stories that she was not very proud of. Stephenie became discouraged and stopped.

Stephenie and Christiaan were married midway through her senior year. Stephenie was quite happy with the decision to marry and saw it as the next logical step in her life and, perhaps, as a balm to tamp out the fires of her creative urges. Because while she remained fearful about exercising her creative thoughts, the idea that she might someday get over that hurdle would not go away.

Stephenie graduated with a degree in English from Brigham Young University in 1996. There were not many options for an English degree. The obvious one was teaching, but teaching did not really hold any appeal for her. The reality was Stephenie had a degree, but was at a loss as to what to do with it.

And so she quite naturally moved into the role of wife. The couple moved into a home in Cave Creek, not too far from where her parents now lived. Christiaan was moving along nicely in his career as an auditor. Wanting to help out with family finances, Stephenie took a job as a receptionist for a local real estate agent. And now there was more than enough time for her to read. Stephenie was adapting quite easily to the married life.

About a year into their marriage, Stephenie discovered that she was pregnant with the couple's first child. The nine months of pregnancy were a lot of good experiences punctuated by one moment of sheer terror that she related during an Entertainment Weekly interview on www.ew.com.

At one point during the pregnancy, doctors informed Stephenie that it appeared she was in real danger of having a miscarriage. A week later doctors informed her that they had made a mistake and the fetus was fine. For Stephenie that was her first real moment of terror and she would always live with the memory and, some have speculated, that it may have subconsciously informed her approach to her vampire saga, especially in the novel *Breaking Dawn*.

After the birth of the couple's first child, Stephenie made the decision to turn any ambition she had at that point in one direction—to that of being a good wife and mother.

And so upon the birth of their first child, a boy they named Gabe, Stephenie gave up the only adult job she would ever have and officially became a full-time mother.

And things pretty much went along that way for the next nine years. Stephenie was quite content with the simple things in life: husband, children, family, friends, and all things centered around the church. Recreation included the occasional movie and family get-togethers. As the years went by, two more children, Seth and Eli, enlarged the family and the challenges of her daily life.

"I was a housewife, raising my three children with my husband," she recalled in an interview with RTÉ Entertainment on www.rte.ie. "We lived just down the road from the school where my kids would go. It was a normal, everyday life."

Stephenie, who once jokingly described her three boys as "monkeys on crack" in the most loving way, had settled into a comfortable routine. She had joined a scrapbooking group, which satisfied her creative and social outlet, and found solace, as always, in a good book. Although the good book was often an awkward scenario with a book and a child balanced on her lap.

Christiaan and Stephenie would occasionally have a difference of opinion, but it was usually about the simple things that married couples disagree about and those were easily resolved. Stephenie had often referred to Christiaan as her soul mate, a cliché description that, in the case of the young couple, was accurate.

Life for Stephenie was good. Until the year 2002.

It had been a rough year for the Meyer family and Stephenie in particular.

During her pregnancy with her third child, Eli, Stephenie had fallen and suffered a severely broken arm. Five weeks after the fall, Christiaan was diagnosed with Crohn's disease (an inflammation of the digestive tract). She was finding her scrapbooking group to be less and less fulfilling on a creative level. But the worst of it all was that Stephenie was uncomfortably aware that much of her life had flown by in an uneventful manner and that she was getting old.

What Stephenie was going through could be considered depression on any number of levels. Concern over her husband's illness. The pressures of raising three children, and the never-ending drain of her physical and mental energy that brings. But at her core, Stephenie had a handle on what the problem was.

"It wasn't a great time in my life," she confessed to *Phoenix New Times*. "I'd put on so much weight with the last two babies. My thirtieth birthday was coming up and I was so not ready to face being thirty. I didn't feel I had much going for me."

four

Bump in the Night

And then there was her creative frustration that was once again bubbling just below the surface. She had tried painting for a time, but that ultimately did not turn out to be the creative outlet she was hoping for. Scrapbooking was more a social outlet than anything really challenging. And there was the smattering of short story fragments, started but quickly discarded in a wave of discouragement.

Stephenie was at a loss. The ideal life she had envisioned for herself had come to pass and, for the longest time, she had been content to live out her life in such a manner. The feelings toward her husband and children had not changed. What had changed was the all-encompassing fulfillment she felt in a happy, largely uneventful family situation. Now she found herself looking around the edges of her existence and searching for something else.

"I loved my kids but I needed something extra, my way to be me," she told the *Arizona Republic*. "I did feel like something was missing."

Adding to her creative woes was the fact that it had just turned summer in Cave Creek, Arizona, and with summer came the onset of one of her worst fears—kids and swimming pools. She was sensitive to the fact that every year there were reports of children drowning in swimming pools and, despite the fact that all of her boys were reasonably good swimmers by age two and were always supervised when in the water, the fear of children drowning had never really left her and had now suddenly intensified.

Throw in the fact that on June 1, 2003, Stephenie was on the first day of her latest diet in an ongoing attempt to lose the baby fat and that the next day the boys were off for their first day of swimming lessons. It was little wonder that Stephenie was in an uneasy mood when she went to bed that night.

At 4:00 A.M. on June 2, 2003, Stephenie awoke from a fitful sleep with memories of a very vivid dream. The particulars of that dream have been the subject of just about every interview Stephenie has ever done but nowhere does it play out more clearly than on her own Web site, www.stepheniemeyer.com.

"In my dream, two people were having an intense conversation in a meadow in the woods," she explained. "One of these people was just your average girl. The other person was fantastically beautiful, sparkly, and a vampire. They were discussing difficulties inherent in the facts that a) they were falling in love with each other while b) the vampire was particularly attracted to the scent of her blood, and was having a difficult time restraining himself from killing her immediately."

Stephenie has indicated in the past that this was not the first time she had dreamed in story form and that she had always had story ideas that she was thinking about. But this dream was something different.

Stephenie remembered the dream as "very vivid" and felt herself "an observer" as she stayed in bed with her eyes closed, mentally dissecting the dream from every possible emotional and psychological angle.

"I can still see it," she explained in a *Courier-Mail* interview. "It was a very unusual dream and I've never had any like it, before or since."

And unlike dreams she's had in the past, which held only mild interest and were gone with the sun, Stephenie was immediately fixated on this vision and could not let it go.

"It was like reading a great book that you don't want to put down," she recalled in a *Phoenix New Times* interview. "You want to know what happens next. So I just laid there imagining."

But eventually the sun came up on the day and Stephenie put the dream aside to get her kids ready for swimming lessons, see to everybody's breakfast, and get her husband off to work. As she went about these mundane chores and household duties, her mind was never far from the dream and what would happen next. Stephenie became so fixated on it that by the time breakfast had been served, she had snuck off to the computer and, with the hustle and bustle of her family forming a constant hum of background noise, she typed out the sentence . . .

In the sunlight he was shocking.

She was struck by the power of the sentence and the potential in that sentence for more. Most important, the sentence that would kick off the dream that would become chapter thirteen of her first book had come from her. There was power in those words, the power of her emotion finally found a crack in her wall of insecurity . . . and had seeped out.

Then she reluctantly grabbed up her kids and drove them off for their swimming lessons. However, for one of the rarest of times, Stephenie's mind was not on her children or their activities. All she could think about was the dream, the vampire and the mortal, and what came next.

After swimming lessons, she made lunch for her children and then made a beeline for the computer. She was ready to type. But then her youngest son, Eli, wanted to be with his mother. Stephenie picked him up and cradled him under one arm, doing an uneasy balancing act as she contemplated what would happen next to her fictional lovers.

"Part of me was shocked at what I was doing," she recalled in a YouTube video. "But I just had to keep going with it. I knew I had to jump right into it because having three kids, I was prone to having short memory, so I felt I had to get it down while it was all fresh in my mind."

There was a bit of hesitation as she faced the screen. Writing what even she realized at that point was a legitimate flight of fancy was something she had not thought of attempting in quite some time. There was an emotional tug-of-war going on as her hands came to rest on the keyboard. Part of her was thinking, Why bother? But a side of her psyche she had not tapped in years was thinking that she did not want to lose the dream and whatever would become of it.

Her fingers tapped the keys. The blank screen began to fill. By the end of that first writing stint, she had completed ten pages. She was hooked. To her way of thinking Stephenie had to find out where the dream would take her if she had not awakened from it. Or if she actually had.

"Once I started on within that day, I was completely hooked on writing," she told a www.collider.com reporter. "All of a sudden I just found it. All of a sudden there it was. I had never dreamed about vampires or had any interest in them. But then I was in and then I had to just keep going with it."

Stephenie was excited, but also cautious at the prospect of taking her dream to its logical conclusion. In her mind, whatever resulted, nobody would ever read it but her. Her long dominant insecurity was speaking. The idea of writing anything with the goal of seeing it published was too much pressure for Stephenie to endure as she attempted to do what she once thought was impossible.

And in line with that attitude, Stephenie adopted a writing process that was nothing if not clandestine. Nobody would know what she was doing. Because in her fragile state, it would only take an offhand comment or even the knowledge that somebody else knew to derail the creative train. For what would turn out to be the next three months, Stephenie would balance her life as wife and mother with a very big secret. And it would not be easy. Her writing time was dictated largely by her children and their schedule.

"I wasn't giving up time with my kids," she told *Collider*. "And I couldn't give up the things I had to do."

However, as the weeks went by and she became increasingly obsessed with the story that was suddenly turning into a full-blown novel, she did find herself becoming increasingly impatient with the mundane things, including the needs of her children, that were taking her away from what she desired most.

"Every time the kids needed something, it was pretty bad," she confessed during a *CBS News Sunday Morning* interview. "I'd be like 'Ugh! I have to get up and get him an apple and that line I was thinking about was so good.'"

But that did not mean that Stephenie was not working on the novel. When she was at the kids' swim lessons or doing chores and errands, she was also mentally stockpiling ideas and thoughts that were destined for her story. Then she would take every opportunity to steal away to the computer and write. She took to writing on scraps of paper when thoughts came to her. There was the very real concern on Stephenie's part that if she did not get a thought down as soon as it came to her, that she would most certainly lose it.

It was during the early writing phase that Stephenie would slip on her headphones and allow her favorite music to guide and influence her thoughts. By now, a near fanatic when it came to new music, the soundtrack that guided her through the maze of emotions she put into *Twilight* included, "Why Does It Always Rain on Me?" by Travis, "Creep" by Radiohead, "I'm Not Okay (I

Promise)" by My Chemical Romance, and "Time Is Run-ning Out" by Muse.

Stephenie had discovered early on that she could not write in silence.

That her husband Christiaan was not immediately suspicious of his wife's actions comes as a bit of a sur-prise. Because Stephenie was spending all her free mo-ments during the day and any number of nights writing, eventually he began to get a little irritated at the fact that his wife seemed to be on the computer all the time. She would not give him a direct answer and she has often indicated that there was some tension in the marriage because of her secrecy.

Stephenie recalled in a *New York Times* interview that the secrecy of what she was doing was beginning to rub her normally easygoing husband the wrong way. "There were times when he would really get mad. He would say 'You never sleep! You don't talk to me! I never get to use the computer!'"

Stephenie was tempted in the face of her husband's irritation and confusion to let him in on her little secret, but decided against it.

"I didn't tell him what I was doing," Stephenie told the *Courier-Mail*. "So he was mystified and a little irri-tated that I was hogging the computer all the time. I just had a hard time telling him that I was writing a story about vampires."

A big reason Stephenie may have had for not revealing the true nature of what she was doing was that perhaps she was having a hard time coming to grips with it herself. She was basically a stranger to the vampire mythos and once, at the suggestion of her husband, had attempted to sit through the vampire movie *The Lost Boys*, but could not make it through. It had been too bloody, too violent, and, yes, too adult for her sensibilities. And then there was the question of romance. In her heart she almost certainly had a picture of what courtship, love, and romance were all about. But to fictionalize it and transport those emotions into a world populated by vampires and werewolves . . . she seemed not quite sure where she stood with all that and so seemed to feel it her duty to keep it to herself.

The writing continued at a pretty much roller-coaster pace. She would always manage to get something down. To her way of thinking, a bad day was only a page or two. On a good day she might finish a chapter and, maybe, start on the next one. One thing she found as the days and weeks went by, and the stack of pages grew higher and higher, was that whether she liked it or not, she could get by on little or no sleep. It seemed a small sacrifice for the creative good. But even Stephenie had her limits and on those nights when her eyes blurred and her mind fogged over, she would reluctantly drag herself to bed.

This was at a time when her youngest was not sleeping through the night and so she was often roused from
even a few moments sleep by the sound of Eli crying.
It was often at these moments that an idea or notion of
what the characters should do or say next would pop
into her head and she would race downstairs and back
to the computer.

Fearing that this lack of sleep would eventually catch
up with her, and fearing it might affect her child-care
skills, she began leaving a pen and notebook by the bed
so she could scrawl an idea down in the middle of the
night for use the next day.

The importance of the book began taking precedence
over anything that was not a necessity in Stephenie's
life. She stopped going to her scrapbooking group.
Movie night was now out of the question because it was
three hours away from the book that she felt she could
not afford to lose. Stephenie was not calling siblings and,
even though they only lived a couple of blocks away, she
was being unavailable to her parents.

"It wasn't like me to be so focused," she told a www.
bookpage.com interviewer.

However, it all seemed worth it to Stephenie because
slowly but surely what had originally been a stack of
pages was beginning to look like a real novel. And, perhaps because of her naïveté when it came to the writing
process, she was taking a rather unorthodox approach

to the book. Rather than start at the beginning of the story, Stephenie began writing at the point of the dream and worked her way forward to the end. Then she went back and wrote the beginning until it matched up with the rest of the book.

Writing the novel was only half the challenge. Creating locations, characters, and even characters' names were things she had to deal with as the pages began to pile up well into the hundreds. For starters she knew absolutely nothing about vampires and their lore and what would or would not work within the context of the story. But rather than research everything there was to know about vampires and try to shoehorn those ideas into the story, she went with what little she did know and basically adapted it her way.

Blood drinking was central to the makeup of her vampires, but in her fantasy world it was easy for her to make her vampires more civilized creatures who drank animal blood rather than human blood, yet, as we found out, could be tempted by the scent of a human. That they never aged and remained, in this case, teens forever played into the romance and intrigue of young love. Stephenie felt her creations could be heroic and romantic and yet not cynical and bored (a staple in many modern vampire tales), which proved to be the icing on the cake.

For the early stages of her writing, Stephenie simply

referred to her main characters as "he" and "she." But when it came time for her to actually name her characters, she looked first to her literary roots and then to her own personal favorites. For Edward she channeled the works of Jane Austen and Charlotte Brontë and came up with a name that was very much of that time, but still relevant in the context of a modern-day romantic fantasy. For Bella it was as simple as borrowing the name Isabella, which is the name she always felt she would call a daughter if she had one.

An issue that had her doing a bit of self-analysis was whether the character of Bella was really Stephenie trying to live a life she did not have through the character and this fictional world. In an interview posted on www.newmoonmovie.org, Stephenie addressed that issue.

"Bella and I think completely differently," she explained. "When I went to write this, it wasn't something I wrote about. But I think it's really natural that I created a character that let me live a life I didn't know because why would I write something I've already experienced."

Stephenie conceded in the interview that while she did bring a few things from her life experience to the character, Bella was much more mature than she was at that age.

"I was really sheltered and she had to be grown-up all of the time. I kind of admire that when I see that in people around me."

Coming up with Forks, Washington, as the setting for the tale was as easy as going online. Stephenie Googled for the place that had the most annual rainfall in the United States and came up with the Olympic Peninsula in Washington State. A further search for the smallest town she could find in the area brought up Forks. Simple as that.

As envisioned by Stephenie, the book was not intended to be a young adult novel, but as she delved deeper into the writing process, it was gradually becoming just that. That Bella arrived in Forks as the result of a personal family situation struck directly at the heart of youthful angst. Her status as the outsider at her new school was very much that. Falling for another outsider, albeit a strangely mysterious and handsome one, stepped lightly and accurately through the overriding theme of young love.

Then came the conundrum—Bella's discovery that Edward is a vampire and a very different one at that. But they overcome the odds and, in a very Romeo and Juliet manner, take the first tentative steps towards making it work. Outside forces intrude. Edward saves Bella's life. They go to the prom. She tells Edward she wants to go to the dark side, to be with him always. Edward refuses.

There were a lot of classic soap opera elements to what Stephenie was doing, classic images that we have read countless times before. But the edges of what could have easily been a period piece were sharp with the rel-evancy of here and now. Stephenie had somehow gotten it right.

This would turn out to be the perfect first book. More teen angst than anyone could shake a stick at. Some mild horror and ultimately a tearjerker of an end-ing. Nothing is perfect, but Stephenie's maiden literary voyage would turn out to be pretty darn close.

Stephenie burned through the remainder of the novel well into the later days of August. When the dust finally settled she had written a 498-page manuscript totaling somewhere in the vicinity of 130,000 words. It had not been any easy ride.

She conceded only half-jokingly on several occasions that she most likely lost some friends during the writ-ing process; not willing to share her secret with family and friends had put a strain on her immediate family. And the toughest part for Stephenie was that once fin-ished with the manuscript, she found she had not got-ten the world of her imagination out of her system.

She has gone into much detail on the hand-wringing post-*Twilight* on her own Web site and in countless in-terviews. The long and short of it was that she had not gotten the odyssey of Edward and Bella to play itself out within the context of a single book. There were, to her way of thinking, a whole lot of things that needed to be addressed. And so while she had begun editing the *Twilight* manuscript, she was simultaneously writing several what she termed "epilogues," essentially simple outlines of where the story should go next. It wasn't long before Stephenie began writing the second book.

Without knowing what the future of the first would be.

"I expected that no one would ever read it except for me," she told the *Courier-Mail*.

But as it turned out, somebody else already had.

five

No Secrets from Emily

Emily Rasmussen knew something was wrong.

Stephenie had been extremely close to her older sister since childhood. They had been each other's confidantes in matters big and small throughout their lives. When Emily married, moved to Utah, and started a family of her own, they were constantly on the telephone for hours on end, alternately serious and giggly as two sisters could be. Their relationship was a central point in their lives; predictable in the most loving kind of way.

And so during the summer of 2003, when the calls became less frequent and then stopped and Stephenie's often chatty e-mails became nonexistent or, at best, extremely vague, Emily became concerned. Emily could only guess that something awful had happened in her younger sister's life that had caused the sudden chill in their relationship. And when she began hearing from family and friends in Cave Creek that Stephenie had become almost a recluse, she decided to take matters into her own hands.

"It was completely abnormal that she wasn't talking to me," recalled Emily in a *Daily Herald* interview. "It was like she had dropped off the face of the earth. So I called her and said, 'What's going on?'"

Stephenie did not know what to say. She had never been one to keep secrets from her older sister. But to her, this was a different situation. She was not very far into the writing at that point. She had no idea how her sister would react if she told her that she was writing a story about vampires and adolescent love. Stephenie was not in the frame of mind to have the book put-down or dismissed. And even worse to her way of thinking was the fear that Emily might quite simply laugh at her. Stephenie knew that a lot was riding on what she did or did not tell her sister.

But, she reasoned, she had never kept secrets from Emily before and now did not seem to be the time to start. She also felt that, just maybe, she needed a sounding board for what she was doing, somebody who could be critical in an honest sort of way. So she took a deep breath and told her sister she was writing a novel.

Emily's response was immediate and enthusiastic.

"When she asked me what was wrong, I said 'Well, I'm kind of writing this story,'" Stephenie told the Sunday *New York Times*. "She said, 'So let me see it!'"

Stephenie took a deeper breath and told her sister what the story was about.

Being a fan of the television series *Buffy the Vampire Slayer*, Emily was totally into what her sister was trying to do. Stephenie felt that Emily would give her an honest opinion. After some sisterly prodding, Stephenie finally agreed to e-mail her a couple of chapters.

She was still at the insecure stage in what she was doing, but felt she was on safe ground with Emily. However, she related in a *Vogue* magazine interview, there was still a lingering fear as she sent her sister those first chapters.

What if she did not like it? What if she thought it was badly written? And, for Stephenie, the worst fear of all: "What if it was all completely stupid?"

She need not have worried. Emily was instantly and totally enraptured by the early images of Edward, Bella, and the mist-shrouded town of Forks. She was immediately on the phone and bombarding her with e-mails asking for more, Stephenie recalled in an entry on her Web site that her sister became "my cheerleading section."

Confident that her sister would be supportive of her creative endeavors, Stephenie began sending out new chapters as fast as her sister would request them.

Of course this was all done after Emily promised that her writing venture would be just their little secret.

When Stephenie had literally written the last line of *Twilight* (then going under the working title of *Forks*), she found herself mentally trying to figure out what to do next.

"I didn't think of publishing until I wrote the very last line," she recalled on www.motleyvision.org. "I had no expectations or direction."

But there was a part of her that felt she owed something to the characters and the story she had created and that, on a purely emotional level, it suddenly seemed important for her to get her creation out into the world.

Again she turned to Emily for advice. Her older sister insisted that she look into getting the novel published. Stephenie thought about it for a long time. Part of her would have felt quite happy if nobody ever read it but herself or maybe her boys when they were old enough, but she continued to struggle with the almost childlike urgency, and no small amount of ego, to get her book published.

And so she embarked on an Internet odyssey, designed to educate herself as to every aspect of the book publishing business. On more than one occasion she has acknowledged that the more she found out about how books were published and the business of book publishing, the more intimidated she became. But she pressed on.

"I knew absolutely nothing about how to get a book published and the more I started reading things about queries and how to get an agent, the more discouraged I became," she said in a YouTube interview. "I almost quit a couple of times but Emily kept encouraging me to keep at it."

By this time, word was officially out that Stephenie had written a novel and that it was about vampires and young love. Family members, especially husband Christiaan, were amazed, but ultimately proud and supportive. Outside her immediate circle, those in the Mormon community were surprised and, by degrees, shocked that somebody so entwined in the Mormon faith would write "one of those kinds of books." It should be noted that almost all of those early opinions were based on secondhand information and that nobody save Emily had actually read the manuscript.

Stephenie, with the aid of several *Writer's Market* guides, had decided that the best way to go was to approach smaller publishing houses that indicated they would accept unsolicited submissions. She also decided to query a few literary agencies as well, discovering that a manuscript by an unknown was usually taken more seriously when an agent represented it. Stephenie sent out a total of fifteen queries. She was not really confident at that point, saying on her Web site that she felt that her query letters "really sucked" and that mailing them "was terrifying."

To this day the moment she dropped those query packages in a corner mailbox remains, by her own estimation in a *National Post* interview, one of her bravest acts.

"Whenever I'm in that part of town, I'll drive by that mailbox where I mailed out those queries and remember that moment all over again. It was probably one of the hardest things I'd ever done; knowing you're going to get rejected and that it's going to hurt."

Christiaan remained supportive of his wife, but he suddenly turned less than enthusiastic when Stephenie announced that she was taking the step of launching her manuscript into the publishing world. After so many years together, Christiaan was keenly aware of Stephenie's feelings and, especially, her sensitivity. Dealing with possible rejection was something he was not looking forward to seeing in his wife.

"He wasn't very enthusiastic because he was trying to protect me," she said in a Sunday *New York Times* interview. "He knew how hard I would take rejection. I think he was concerned that I was going to get hurt."

Mentally, Stephenie's mind was on the queries and she would be the first to the mailbox every day in search of any kind of response. The possible scenarios were playing a constant loop in her head. Within a short period of time, responses to her queries began coming back.

"I had the easiest publishing experience in the whole world," she related to www.collider.com. "I sent out fifteen letters, got five no replies, nine rejections, and one that said I want to see it."

The one positive response came from an assistant at the agency called Writers House. The irony was the agency was a last-minute addition to her mailing list at the suggestion of her younger sister, Heidi, who had read on the Web site of a famous writer that Writers House was a good place to approach for representation.

Writers House requested the first three chapters. Stephenie was concerned because she did not consider the first three chapters the strongest elements of the book. And so she was happily surprised a few weeks later when she received a letter from Writers House requesting the entire manuscript. Agent Jodi Reamer received the manuscript and started to read.

"I took it home that night because I usually don't read in the office," she told the *Daily Herald*. "I read until 3 A.M. I spent the whole next day thinking about the manuscript and wishing the day was over so I could go home and read it. By the time I finished reading, I knew I could sell it."

Over the next few days, Stephenie contemplated the

fate of *Twilight* as she went about her daily routine and tried to maintain some semblance of a normal family life and to continue, at a more leisurely pace, to work on the second book, *New Moon*. But what the agent was thinking was never far from her mind.

With the cat quite literally out of the bag, Stephenie was suddenly a minor celebrity in the town of Cave Creek. Christiaan and the boys were now tolerant of her time spent at the computer. There were the inevitable "What's going to happen in the next book?" and "Have you heard from the agent?" questions Stephenie did not have the answers to. All she could do was wait.

A few days later she received a phone call from agent Jodi Reamer. She had read the book, loved it, and wanted to represent Stephenie. Stephenie remembered little of the conversation outside of the fact that she tried real hard to play it cool and professional, but that she didn't think she was fooling anybody.

The next two weeks were spent in long distance conversations and e-mails as Stephenie and Jodi worked on the editing phase of the manuscript. The title was officially changed from *Forks* to *Twilight* and a few rough patches were smoothed out.

That the manuscript clocked in at nearly five hundred pages did not seem to concern anybody. There was the suggestion that Edward and Bella engage in premarital sex at some point. Stephenie put her foot down and said that was not in keeping with the spirit of the book and she would not do it. The subject was instantly dropped.

Stephenie's decision was much more than merely her insistence on preserving the integrity of the story. It was an example, one that would surface often, of the strength of her moral compass. The book deal and a whole lot of money would not have meant much if she was going to have to compromise her principles. She had no idea how the publishing business worked. But she knew how she worked.

Stephenie admitted in a www.mtv.com interview some years later that she was totally without experience when it came to the publishing world and so was easily intimidated by the editors and publishers.

"I felt like I was a kid in school and the principal was telling me what to do," she recalled. "It was hard for me. There were things I changed in that first story that I sometimes think that maybe would have been better if I hadn't. What really unleashed the lioness waiting inside was when they tried to mess with who my characters were. If it was something threatening the characters, I could hold my own."

When Reamer was satisfied that the manuscript was in shape, she sent it out to nine publishers she felt would be interested in this kind of book.

One of those copies ended up in the hands of Megan Tingley, an editor at the publishing house Little, Brown and Company. She began reading the manuscript at the start of a long airplane ride. By the time the flight was over, she was sold.

Tingley would later tell anybody who would listen that it was a combination of desire and danger that drew her into the book. She could not put the book down and was assured that the book would be a success halfway through the reading.

"I could not wait for the plane to land so I could sign up the book," she enthusiastically related to *Phoenix New Times*.

Shortly after Thanksgiving 2003 Stephenie received another call from Reamer. Little, Brown loved the book and was prepared to offer Stephenie a $300,000 three-book deal. Stephenie was speechless. A moment later she went into near shock when she found out that Reamer had not only turned down the offer but jacked Stephenie's asking price up to $1,000,000.

For a moment, Stephenie's mind flashed on this whole process having been one big and very cruel joke that a lot of people she really did not know were playing on her. There was the immediate concern that the agent asking so much would turn publishers off to the book. The emotional roller coaster instantly went the other way when Reamer said Little, Brown had made a counter offer of $750,000 and that if it was okay with her, she would accept it.

"Sometimes I feel so guilty about how this all happened," she told www.bookpage.com. "People go through so much to get published. I skipped over the bad parts. Somehow it feels like cheating."

But once she got over the guilt, Stephenie was soon the kid on Christmas Day who had just gotten the best possible present, as she would explain to *Rolling Stone*. "My life twisted around into 'I have an agent. I have a book deal. I have a career and, wow! I'm going to be a writer.'"

As it turned out, the book deal was not the slam dunk it has been portrayed as in most interviews. The publishing trade, like most entertainment businesses, is notorious for its high turnover rate, especially at the higher end. And what Stephenie did not know at the time was that *Twilight* was submitted to a publisher whose ultimate decision maker only had a little time left in office.

In an Internet interview that appeared on the Web site www.examiner.com, Larry Kirschbaum, former head of Time Warner Books, the parent company of Little, Brown and Company, recalled that the notion of signing Stephenie to a three-book deal for a huge amount of money was a huge risk for the company for any author, let alone a housewife who had never published before.

"When the book by Stephenie Meyer was submitted to us toward the end of my stay at Time Warner, it was a very, very large deal. It was three books for six figures and it was a significant six figures. And I was very skeptical."

But the publishing head ended up doing what he nearly always did, which was to trust his editors and their gut feelings. And so when everybody he talked to indicated the deal would provide a major upside for the company, he crossed his fingers and signed off on it.

Stephenie summoned up her last amount of cool and said she would love that. As soon as she hung up the phone, she began wandering around her home, seemingly in a daze, and laughing hysterically.

It had easily been the most amazing six months of her life. It had started with a dream. It had ended in a dream. Stephenie was now a soon-to-be-published author.

And she could not stop laughing.

Because her book was actually going to wind up in bookstores.

"And people were actually going to pay me for doing something that I was doing for fun," she said in a YouTube video.

six

Start . . . Stop . . . Start

Needless to say, Christmas 2003 was a bit more joyous than usual. Stephenie was constantly beaming at the idea that her creative dreams had come true so quickly. But while she was beside herself with joy, Stephenie was about to learn that the wheels of publishing moved slowly.

The reality is that it is the rare book that goes from author to bookstore in less than a year. And eighteen months or longer is not uncommon. And with a marketing and promotion plan just getting off the ground at Stephenie's publisher, the anxious author was just going to have to wait.

Barely into 2004, Little, Brown had decided for a fall 2005 release of *Twilight*. And while Stephenie was already chafing at the prospect of waiting so long to see *Twilight* on bookshelves, she was beginning to at least tolerate the fact that the book world did not move at lightning speed.

"I've gotten impatient from time to time," she re-called, looking back on those prepublication days on one of her Web site entries. "But I'm glad I've had the last two years to try and come to terms with the situation. I'm greatly looking forward to finally having *Twilight* on the shelves and more than a little frightened too."

In an attempt to keep her mind off her sudden writing notoriety and to satisfy her curiosity about the town she had picked off the Internet to set her book, Stephenie and her sister Emily made a low-key trip to Forks in the summer of 2004. Stephenie was in the mood for a bit of sightseeing and had not been to Washington before. It was also a chance to spend some quality time with her sister who at the time was seven months pregnant. But she was also concerned that the Forks of her imagination might not be the Forks of reality.

Happily the two days spent walking the streets of the real Forks, seeing the buildings and talking to the people, ultimately assured her that she had gotten Forks right. She would continue to be diligent in her research of the town, looking up maps and studying surveys and reports on the topography and the geology of the area to make sure that her fantasy version and the reality of the town meshed.

Given their investment in Stephenie, it came as no surprise that the publisher wasted no time in getting out the word on their major new literary find. The initial dream, the writing process, and the miraculous turn of events that led to the Little, Brown deal were natural publicity fodder and the story was soon the talk of the publishing world. Because the reality was that getting a book published in this day of economic woes had gotten increasingly difficult and the almost fairy-tale ease with which Stephenie had arrived on the scene was a story worth covering.

Select copies were circulated to tastemakers in both the book and film community and it was not long before a film deal was struck for *Twilight*.

Paramount Pictures in association with MTV Films had made the initial option offer for the film rights to *Twilight*. Stephenie had always written in what she described as a "visual style" and was excited at the prospect of her creation ending up on the big screen. And she was quick to exploit the windfall of option money to buy a bright, shiny new toy.

Always a lover of cars and, in particular, the mystery and romance associated with the open road, Stephenie in an interview with www.bookstories.com announced the purchase of a G35 Infiniti coupe with all the extras. "I figured that any money that comes from MTV has to be spent frivolously as a matter of principle. So it's nice to drive something besides the minivan on the rare occasion that I go somewhere without my kids."

In the meantime, Stephenie continued to write.

One of the many epilogues Stephenie had written in the wake of completing *Twilight* had struck her fancy and it was not long before she selected it as the jumping-off point for what would be the continuation of the Edward-Bella saga, *Forever Dawn*.

Admittedly, *Forever Dawn* was written in a transitional phase. *Twilight* had not yet found a publisher. *Twilight* had a clearly defined ending. But probably the biggest fly in the ointment was that Stephenie had never considered that she was writing a young adult book. And without going into too much detail, *Forever Dawn* basically skipped over the latter stages of Bella's high school experience and had moved far enough into the future so that Bella was now dealing with more mature problems and challenges.

It did not take long for Stephenie to understand this, thanks to some subtle suggestions that she might want to stay true to the tone and intent of *Twilight*. Stephenie had on more than one occasion acknowledged a good feeling about where *Forever Dawn* was going, but ultimately decided to put it away.

Stephenie was basically put in the position of having to start over in order to be consistent with her own creation.

But she was never one to leave her manuscripts unfinished. Knowing full well that *Forever Dawn* would never see print, she nevertheless plunged ahead and ultimately finished the 300-page manuscript. She presented *Forever Dawn* to Emily as a gift and has proclaimed to anyone who has asked that nobody else would ever see it.

It was during the time that Stephenie was writing *Forever Dawn* that she had what she considered "a hard-fought battle" with her publisher about how long the *Twilight* series should run and how it should end.

"When I was working on *Forever Dawn*, my publishers told me that it might be a good idea to keep Bella in high school a bit longer and to make the series more young adult," she told a Chicago crowd during her *Breaking Dawn* tour. "Then they told me that they would like me to end the series with *Eclipse* and keep it a happy ending."

Stephenie's response was an emphatic no. She had long since outlined the entire series and its characters to include a fourth book, *Breaking Dawn*. To trim one book would force compromises to the integrity of her original story that she was not ready to make. After what seemed like an eternity of back and forth between Stephenie and Little, Brown and Company, Stephenie got her way.

As she mentally retrenched in preparation for starting a more appropriate follow-up to *Twilight*, she had to tell herself that writing a sequel was much different when you know the first book was going to be published. What kick-started *New Moon* in Stephenie's mind was that the book would open in Bella's senior year and that Edward was nowhere to be found. Then would come the penultimate question.

What happened?

These were challenging times for Stephenie: The impact of having a three-book deal and the fact that the second manuscript would be due at some point. She was also getting some early notices from Little, Brown about some press interviews with important outlets that she would be doing at some point. Being basically shy by nature, Stephenie was looking ahead to those obligations with more than a touch of nervousness.

It helped that, by this time, everybody in her life was well aware of what she was doing. When she had to write, it was easy for Christiaan or her parents to step in and take the kids for a while. That her writing was no longer a deep, dark secret was a huge weight off her shoulders.

But the big hurdle was the process of writing *New Moon*. The author had no outline when she was writing *Twilight*. With *New Moon* she was forced to consider a bit of order in what she was doing.

"I had to start outlining," she disclosed in an interview

with www.about.com. "I knew when I started writing *New Moon* where the story was going to end so I had to do a lot more work to tie up the threads to the story."

Stephenie's change in writing style, by her own admission, had a lot to do with her growing knowledge of how her approach to writing could best fit in with such requirements of mainstream publishing with its deadlines and editors.

Stephenie's approach to writing, which began with *New Moon,* had her first writing what she considered her "ice cream" scenes, those that she was more attracted to than others. Those scenes would, in turn, suggest others. She would then go back and write all the necessary exposition, transitions, and descriptions. There was nothing linear about this newly evolved writing process but, for Stephenie, it was working.

The biggest obstacle to writing *New Moon* was the fact that she had so much emotion invested in these characters. And that at moments during the writing of *New Moon* she would find herself talking to her characters.

Stephenie knew how strange that must have sounded and has always been quick to declare she is not crazy.

But she was so involved with her characters and, in the case of Edward, she was dealing with the heart-wrenching ordeal of his leaving very early in the story line. "I pitched a fit that was very violent and tearful," she offered in her Web site. "It was a bitter pill to swallow."

With Edward out of the picture, Stephenie was then faced with how Bella would deal with the pain of his being gone. She channeled some of the great women and great losses of literature. Juliet in *Romeo and Juliet*. Scarlett O'Hara in *Gone with the Wind*. Through often tearful writing sessions, Stephenie created a Bella who was dogged and determined in the face of loss, yet confident that the love of Edward would always be there and would always be hers.

Stephenie had become more wide-ranging in her musical interests since writing *Twilight*, and *New Moon* was conspicuous by the wide array of modern rock and pop that was propelling and influencing the writing of her second novel. Stephenie's playlist this time around included such songs as "Do You Realize?" by The Flaming Lips, "Be My Escape" by Relient K, "Never Let You Down" by Verve Pipe, and the perennial Muse tune "Apocalypse Please."

Midway through 2004, Stephenie felt she had *New Moon* at a place where she liked it. But she sensed there might be some pitfalls ahead. Would young readers be patient enough to go through the portion of the story in which Edward was not around or would they just skim through those pages and only begin to read again when Edward appeared?

Loyalty to the story as well as the characters was a chance Stephenie was willing to take as she shipped *New Moon* off to Little, Brown.

In hindsight, *New Moon* was a very risky book on so many fronts, it is no wonder that it has turned out to be the most controversial of the series. The very early on attempt on Bella's life that compels Edward and the rest of the Cullen clan to leave Forks immediately put the character interplay of the first book in jeopardy. With Edward out of the picture, the focus is on Bella and her life alone. The thrill-seeking aspects of her turn and her falling in with the alleged wrong crowd, Jacob (a fringe character in *Twilight* now given full sway) and the werewolves, are never less than interesting, but, for those readers into the more gradual seduction and atmosphere of *Twilight*, the result is jarring and, by degrees, off-putting.

Edward's journey to Italy and his dealings with Volturi are effective and move the story along nicely, but, taken within the context of the story in *New Moon*, almost seems to belong in another story. Fortunately things seem to get back on more familiar ground once Edward returns to Forks and the ongoing question of change wraps things up in a quite satisfying and quietly suspenseful manner.

Although she would continue to write throughout the remainder of 2004, the pace was leisurely enough to allow her to return to her favored role of housewife and mother. Sundays had remained hers even throughout the hectic last year and she had continued to find peace in her weekly three hours at church and with the church-related teaching she had begun doing.

She would occasionally get calls and e-mails from her agent and from Little, Brown. There was the excitement of early renderings of what would become the cover of *Twilight*. News was also forthcoming that a writer was being sought to do a first draft of the script and that Paramount-MTV was anxious to greenlight the picture for production as soon as possible.

Into 2005, Stephenie was slowly, but surely, rounding into shape in terms of dealing with the media and making public appearances. She has admitted to being very nervous during those early press outings and, she explained, she was often close to throwing up before several of them. But she gradually became more comfortable in front of reporters and adoring crowds. She began to stammer less and found herself evolving into a confident and assured spokesperson for her creation.

The popular press, always looking for an angle to hang a new pop culture icon on, was quick to make the comparison between Stephenie and J. K. Rowling whose Harry Potter books had caught the world by surprise and whose run was at midpoint of a series that had sold untold millions.

Stephenie could see no basis in the comparison outside of the fact that they were both women and that their books were fantasy oriented. She praised Rowling and quietly speculated that it would be nice for her books to do as well as Rowling's have done. But in no way was she ready to proclaim herself the second coming of Rowling, something the popular press seemed more than happy to do for her.

Stephenie's relatively quiet time post–*New Moon*'s completion came to an end when it was announced that *Twilight* would be in stores on October 5, 2005. Taking a cue from the Rowling campaigns, several bookstores were planning special in-store events to herald the unveiling of *Twilight*. But, admittedly, as Stephenie counted down the days to *Twilight* being in stores, she was blissful with the knowledge that this was the end of a dream that had started with a dream.

Twilight was brought into the world on October 5, 2005. The book was greeted with much anticipation from the young adult crowd (the book's seemingly intended audience). But those who looked for trends were quick to notice that the mothers of the daughters were also showing an interest in the book.

Early reviews were primarily positive. Even those that were mixed, and that found some flaws in character, dialogue, and a story line that seemed a bit too heavy-handed for its own good, were equally adamant that the book would be hard to resist.

Publishers Weekly immediately anointed Stephenie "one of the most promising new authors of 2005." *The New York Times* enthused, "The book perfectly captures the teenage feeling of sexual tension and alienation." The reviewer for the *Post and Courier* said, "*Twilight* gripped me so fiercely that I called the nearest teenager and begged for her copy after I misplaced mine."

Stephenie had received her author's copies of *Twilight* shortly before the publication date. And one of the first to get a signed copy and a great big thank-you was Professor Steven Walker from Brigham Young.

"I was thrilled when she sent me an early copy of *Twilight*," he recalled. "I read it the night it came and sent her back a brief note, celebrating the success of it and, as it turned out, her meteoric rise to fame."

Within a month of its release *Twilight* made its debut on the *New York Times* Best Seller List at number five. It would eventually peak at number one and would ultimately stay on the Best Seller List for an almost unheard of ninety-one weeks. The book would also be named one of *Publishers Weekly*'s Best Children's Books of 2005. By 2009, *Twilight* will have reached seventeen million copies sold.

There were more interviews and, as the questions

were often repeated and expected, Stephenie became quite adept at answering them. She easily explained that *Twilight* was not really a horror novel despite the presence of vampires. She offered that, yes, there were elements of Mormon philosophy in the story line, but that it was not a strictly Mormon book. She talked incessantly about the dream and how it had flowered into the book. She occasionally got tired of the media requests but, with rare exception, handled them all like a pro. And the reason was that this was all new to her and all very exciting.

The hysteria surrounding *Twilight* was slow in coming at that point. But the signs were there in how reporters were equating this as something other than a first novel from an unknown writer. Not surprisingly teenage girls were all over the concept of the vampire-human romance. It resonated in a way that, as she would later find out, reflected their own hopes and dreams. The story was their own and, when the screams, applause, and, yes, tears came, it was obvious that so was Stephenie.

For Stephenie, in the days and weeks that followed the publication of *Twilight*, it was all about the small moments in what continued to be her fairly simple days in Cave Creek. She would still find time to drive around town and dine at her favorite restaurant. She was gracious when approached by people who offered shy congratulations, compliments on the book, or the request for an autograph.

It would be those small moments that Stephenie would savor the most. The people who knew her before she became a writer were largely low-key in their praise. There was little if any hysteria or the acknowledgment of celebrity. Stephenie quite simply saw it as their acknowledgment of a friend who had done something out of the ordinary but who was still nothing less than a friend.

Fellow churchgoers were still somewhat divided on this writer in their ranks. Some were a bit skeptical of this good Mormon woman who had written this sexy book about vampires. Those who had actually read the book and were more progressive in their thinking still pretty much thought of her as Stephenie, the member of the church who had written a very interesting book.

Stephenie's church took a very evenhanded approach to its most celebrated member. It did not matter what religion she was and her religion did not weigh into their feelings about the books and its author. The head of the congregation did, almost matter-of-factly, indicate that both his wife and daughter were fans of Stephenie's books.

Stephenie's parents and family members had been totally supportive of their daughter's writing and, for Stephen and Candy, their support manifested itself in a full display of the book situated just inside their front door for all visitors to see.

For Stephenie, easily one of the best moments of her budding literary career came the first time she entered the local bookstore and saw *Twilight* prominently displayed near the front door. A lot of thoughts were going through her head at that moment.

But all she could do was stare and smile.

However, Stephenie was doing more than basking in the glory of *Twilight*. She was already well into outlining the third book in the series. And since fans and publishers alike were making it clear that they would be quite happy for a long Harry Potter kind of franchise, Stephenie began dropping not-too-subtle hints that she had always planned for the odyssey of Edward and Bella to conclude at the end of four books and that, baring a change of circumstance, the fourth book would be the last.

But she was not planning on that being the end of her writing career.

Stephenie had long hinted of a lot of other ideas and those few who had access to the piles of notes scattered in folders and drawers around her work space allegedly saw things that had nothing to do with her romantic vampire saga.

Stephenie obviously had other things up her sleeve.

seven

Lessons Learned

Change is inevitable. When it came to change, Stephenie was fighting it at every turn.

She was convinced that she could continue to lead the life of a normal wife and mother and that the sudden demands brought on by celebrity would not get in the way. And to a degree she was succeeding. Early on she had indicated that she would not do anything book-related on Sunday and, to their credit, Little, Brown, even if they did not completely understand the complexities and nuances of the Mormon religion, abided by her wishes.

But inevitably, the press interviews, the traveling for book signings, and the ever-increasing crowds at larger events began to force her to rethink what a life as a best-selling author would entail. An assistant was brought in to aid Stephenie with her paperwork and the scheduling of events and press interviews. There was talk of a full-time nanny being brought in but, at that point, it was only talk. Stephenie's parents were always available to step in with the kids in an emergency and Christiaan, who remained stalwart in the face of his wife's growing celebrity, never had to be asked twice to help with the kids or the housework.

Stephenie's endearing innocence and naïveté remained well intact but as her popularity rose, she became well aware of things like security and the problems that she might have when security was breached. Little, Brown had been judicious and cautious when it came to passing out advance reading copies of their books and, in the case of *New Moon*, security had been high on their list to avoid leaks of this all-important book.

Unfortunately, one of those copies made it into the hands of a librarian who felt it was her duty to leak spoilers (important plot points) on an Internet site. When Stephenie found out about the leak, she was so upset that she cried for two days. And that's when things really got heated.

"Everyone read it," she told *Phoenix New Times*, "and then they started e-mailing me. I couldn't defend myself so I had to deal with six months of e-mails saying, in all caps, WHY WOULD YOU DO THIS TO ME? It was like being attacked."

That wasn't the end of Stephenie's *New Moon* problems. Sadly it has become a common practice for those with access to advance reading copies of books by top authors to put them on sites like eBay and to sell them for highly inflated collector's prices. The fact that the practice was totally illegal did not prevent several copies of *New Moon* from appearing on eBay with asking prices of several hundred dollars. Little, Brown, for their part, was angry that copies had leaked out under whatever circumstances.

Stephenie's concern was from a more creative place as advance reading copies have usually not been edited completely and she was concerned that people buying these copies would feel ripped off at what they perceived as an inferior written manuscript.

This would not be the only lesson learned by Stephenie. By 2006, she had already been down the classic Hollywood road in regards to the movie version of *Twilight*. Stephenie had gone into the deal with Paramount-MTV with high hopes and the best of intentions. But even as the ink was drying on the option deal, she already knew better.

"I had realized that it could go wrong," she said in an interview with the horror Web site www.bloody-disgusting.com. "And that it could be done very badly."

But even her worst fears could not have prepared her for the script for *Twilight* that had been mailed to her for her inspection. Bella had been transformed into a big-time high school track star. The vampires all wore night vision goggles. As Stephenie painfully recalled, the list of things wrong with that script went on forever. The script for *Twilight* was essentially *Twilight* in name only, devoid of everything that made the book such a joyous experience.

"I got a look at the script," she sighed during a www.about.com interview. "Objectively it was probably a decent vampire movie that had nothing at all to do with *Twilight*. You could have produced that movie and gotten away with giving me no credit because it had nothing to do with the book. It was kind of shocking to me. Maybe it was because I was so naïve that I didn't realize that this stuff happened all the time."

To say that Stephenie was upset with the situation was an understatement.

There were some vague promises by Paramount to do a rewrite, but ultimately the studio did nothing except let the option expire. Almost to the day Paramount let the option lapse, a lesser known but equally potent production company, Summit Entertainment, stepped in and enthusiastically stated that they wanted to make a deal to make the film. In existence since 1989, Summit had built a solid and occasionally blockbuster reputation with a mixture of horror films, major studio outlets, and small, independent films that included *Mr.*

and Mrs. Smith, Memento, Fear and Loathing in Las Vegas,
and American Pie.

Having been burned once already, Stephenie was not
anxious to go down this road again and had already
painted a rather grim scenario as she reluctantly agreed
to hear what Summit had to say.

"I felt I had learned my lesson," she told www.about.
com. "I could tell that if I came to them with a list and
said, 'Okay, these are the things I want,' they would hesi-
tate and put on the brakes. So I really wasn't sure about
this."

Consequently she almost fell out of her chair when
Erik Feig, the president of production at Summit, said
he would draw up a contract guaranteeing that the film
would be true to her vision and that no vampire would
be portrayed as having fangs.

Summit's proposal sounded good. However, so had
Paramount's. So even though the company insisted that
they really wanted to make Twilight and make it right,
Stephenie was still not sure and was seriously thinking
of walking away from the deal. Finally, Stephenie laid it
out to Summit Entertainment in the most blunt, most
un-Hollywood way she could think of.

"Finally I told them, 'What if I give you a list of things
that absolutely cannot be changed?'" she told www.
collider.com. "I ended up giving them a very funda-
mental outline, the basic rules of the vampire world I've

created. Which, to me, meant no fangs, no coffins, they sparkle in the sunlight. The characters have to exist by their present names and their present forms. And finally nobody can be killed who doesn't die in the book. For me, those were just the basic things, the foundation of the story."

On a more personal front, Stephenie added one item to her list of "musts" that was not open to discussion. "I put a clause in my contract that the movie had to be PG-13 so I could go see it," she told a www.timesonline.com reporter.

Stephenie was amazed when, shortly after presenting her demands, the company came back with their promise in writing. In the best possible way, Summit had called her bluff. Stephenie was still not completely sure of this latest proposal, but she had learned enough about how the big studios worked to believe that this was the best opportunity to bring *Twilight* to the screen her way. And so she agreed.

And Summit in those early weeks were as good as their word. Even when there was nothing to report, she was told that. Any proposals for locations and, at this early date, actors for the lead roles of Edward and Bella were passed on to Stephenie. By summer 2006, Stephenie's confidence in the system was improving.

Not long after the deal with Summit was struck, Stephenie was caught up in a whirlwind of obligations to help publicize her forthcoming second book, *New Moon*, which was now scheduled for an August 6, 2006, release. There were the seemingly endless press interviews and, because there was now an increased interest in Stephenie and her books, she was being forced to talk incessantly about the dream, the process by which she was published, and all about being a Mormon writer to the point where she was mentally dizzy from it all. But Stephenie remained professional, patient, and a good sport about it all.

There was also an increasing number of large events in which thousands of fans were given the opportunity to see and hear Stephenie for the first time and to have books signed. It was during these appearances that Stephenie was, for the first time, stunned by the across-the-board appeal her books were having. Standing and screaming elbow to elbow with their teenage daughters were mothers, many well into their forties, some heavily tattooed, and all wearing some kind of T-shirt or jewelry with ties to *Twilight*. When she entered a hall, the shouts of approval were long, lingering, and, yes, quite loud. Stephenie would often remark during this period that she now knew what it was like to be a rock star.

In July 2006 Stephenie made good on a promise she had made upon her initial visit to Forks in 2004 to return for another visit. This time she made it a family affair by bringing along Christiaan and the boys. But more than a mere visit, Stephenie was going to be honored by the local Forks community for the success of her first book, *Twilight*, and for single-handedly putting the small northwestern town on the map.

The Forks community welcomed Stephenie and her family with open arms. They proclaimed July 20, 2006, as Stephenie Meyer Day in conjunction with her visit. Garlic seeds were distributed to residents in a good-natured send-up of her vampire tale and even the chief of police got into the act, dressing up as the fictional Bella's father and presenting Stephenie with a triple-decker peanut butter and jelly sandwich. In return, Stephenie held sway in a reading of *Twilight* and a question-and-answer session in a local park. The party then moved to the town library where Stephenie signed more than two hundred copies of *Twilight* for local fans.

Stephenie enjoyed this working holiday and left with a real kinship with the town and its people. Not long after the visit, the rumor began circulating that Stephenie was looking to buy a summer getaway home somewhere in the Forks township.

Travel had become a big part of her publicity push and it was not limited to just the United States. *Twilight* had sold to many countries overseas where the tale proved equally popular to European readers. And so it was that in May 2006 Stephenie made her first-ever trip outside the United States to the small Italian town of Voltarre in which a scene from *New Moon* takes place. She was amazed to discover that even in that remote town, the square was filled to overflowing with fans who screamed and shouted at the sight of her.

As summer turned to fall, Stephenie was getting some writing done but not as much as she would have liked. Business was the necessary evil that was keeping her from her creative urges that she was still coming to grips with, which was just as well because the fate of *New Moon* was very much on her mind.

New Moon was not the tidy follow-up to *Twilight* that everybody was hoping for. Some chances were being taken that not everybody was going to be happy with. And, to Stephenie's way of thinking, there had been enough leaks to potentially blunt the impact the book would have with her readers.

As always, her fingers were crossed and she hoped for the best.

New Moon's official publication date hit at the stroke of midnight on September 6, 2006. And the resulting mania was just as Stephenie and Little, Brown and Company had hoped for.

There had been quite a bit of hoopla surrounding the previous year's release of *Twilight*, but it could not compare to the fan response to *New Moon*. Bookstores were quick to jump into the spirit of the occasion with many midnight unveilings of the book. Some fans showed up in costumes. Stores could not keep the book on the shelves.

Critically *New Moon*, like the previous *Twilight*, was met with primarily positive, albeit mixed, reviews. Some felt that the writing, especially in the book's introductory chapters, was a bit on the stilted side, with one reviewer comparing Stephenie's writing style to that of the typical Baby-sitter's Club book. Others complained, only mildly, about Edward not being around for a good part of the book.

USA Today praised the book, saying, "*New Moon* piles on the suspense and romance." *Kirkus Reviews* described the book as "An exciting page-turner. This tale of tortured demon lovers entices." *VOYA* announced, "It maintains a brisk pace and near-genius balance of breathtaking romance and action."

For her part, Stephenie had developed a tough hide when it came to reviews. She could be slightly upset when a review was on the cruel or mocking side. But, for the most part, she took the *New Moon* reviews, good and bad, in stride.

New Moon made its debut on the *New York Times* Best Seller List within days and went to number one on the list one week after publication. It would remain on the list for thirty weeks. An example of the international popularity of Stephenie's books came with the announcement by Little, Brown that *New Moon* had shot to the top of the bestseller lists in Germany and Spain.

This kind of response brought a myriad of pundits into the critical arena, espousing different theories. But the most telling one was the one less traveled.

And that was that young people were still reading books.

eight

April and August

Those convinced that success would spoil Stephenie Meyer or, at the very least, turn her into a raving, temperamental diva found the author into late 2006 to be a major disappointment. Because in the face of all the notoriety, Stephenie seemed to be doing her best to maintain a single-minded sense of normalcy.

On any given day in Cave Creek, Arizona, Stephenie, behind the wheel of the long-enduring minivan, could be spotted driving down the street, her boys in tow, heading for swimming lessons, shopping for clothes, or driving across town for a church-related activity. The only outward sign that things might have changed was the occasional glimpse of Stephenie tooling through town behind the wheel of her Infiniti, which usually indicated a few hours off to drive around town or make a quick trip through desert roads. But for the most part one could not imagine that the bliss she reflected in the neighborhood hid an author up-to-here with real-world pressures and deadlines.

"In my everyday, normal life, it's just something I don't think about very much," she explained to the *Seattle Post-Intelligencer*. "I'm still a mom above all else and I'm glad I still get to have a normal life."

But with the end-of-the-year holidays fast approaching, Stephenie was feeling confident and brave in the face of her good fortune. So much so that she unexpectedly decided to take her writing talents in a different, albeit extremely low-profile direction. Stephenie conceived and wrote a religious-oriented story entitled "Hero at the Grocery Store," a touching and heartwarming Christmas tale based on her true-life experiences, for the December 2006 issue of the Latter-day Saints magazine called *Ensign*.

For Stephenie, this simple tale had everything her high-profile novels did not. It was based in a very real, rather than supernatural, setting. Likewise the characters were drawn from a very real-life experience. This was not *Twilight* and that's just the way Stephenie liked it.

The story of a woman who does a charitable favor for a woman struggling to pay her grocery bill was well received by the Mormon community and, until 2008, went unknown by even the most hard-core of Stephenie's fans. For Stephenie it was perceived as a warm and emotionally fulfilling thing before she returned full-time to the business at hand.

Not too long after the story appeared in *The Ensign*, Stephenie was once again drawn into the short story form when she was approached to write a piece for an anthology called *Prom Nights from Hell*. The anthology, which also featured contributions by popular teen authors Meg Cabot, Kim Harrison, Lauren Myracle, and Michele Jaffe, had a premise of lighthearted horror stories about high school proms gone wrong.

Stephenie was intrigued by the invitation, having only marginally played with the short story over the years and never with what she considered real good results. So she took the chance and fashioned the short story entitled "Hell on Earth," the story of a prom night that is nearly destroyed by warring biblical demons. With perhaps more of an aside to her character Edward and a clear homage to her son, a very attractive angel named Gabe arrives on the scene just in time to save the day. The book would hit shelves in April 2007 to favorable reviews.

As with everything Stephenie was doing at this point, the question immediately arose about whether she had designs on expanding the "Hell on Earth" concept into a full-length novel or, like *Twilight*, a new series of books. Stephenie was amused and slightly intrigued at the notion but quickly came to the realization that she already had quite a bit on her plate.

On a much grander but perhaps easier scale, when compared to the previous two books, Stephenie was putting the finishing touches on the third book in the Edward and Bella saga, *Eclipse*. It was easy for a number of reasons. She had for a long time found her voice and rhythm to the series and now it was simply a matter of following the very detailed, long-ago written outline.

Truth be known, given the number of interviews she was giving during this period, there were almost no comments regarding the writing process and very few regarding the story line. In one interview that ran on YouTube, Stephenie was up-front in saying that she did not want to give out too much information about the book. Her silence was perceived to be a not-too-subtle suggestion from Little, Brown in an attempt to build the mystery and anticipation for *Eclipse*. However, the consensus was that Stephenie was still more than a bit gunshy following the leaks that marred the secrecy of *New Moon*.

In hindsight, it is easy to see that, with *Eclipse*, there were signs of a natural maturity by Stephenie as a writer. Whereas in previous books it appeared that Edward and Bella were taking turns in the spotlight, in *Eclipse* they appeared to be on equal footing in their scenes together. The characters and story line were taking all the logical turns in this transitional setup to what would be the final book, but it studiously avoided the pitfalls of formula and contained an expansion of depth, character, and stylings.

It has always been difficult to pick out a best book in a series, especially one with a young adult base. And transitional third books have always been viewed as lesser works designed to do little more than keep things moving. But *Eclipse* arrived as a legitimate, robust addition to the legacy. And, at the end of the day, may have been Stephenie's best-written book to date.

Stephenie's musical accompaniment to *Eclipse* was again far afield. Of course there was Muse. There would always be Muse. But Stephenie had discovered new tunes that fit the mood and subtext of *Eclipse* and added them to the fold as well. These included "Overweight" by Blue October, "Mr. Brightside" by The Killers, "This Is How I Disappear" by My Chemical Romance, and "The Well and the Lighthouse" by her new favorite, Arcade Fire.

Early in 2007, the decision was made for Christiaan to quit his job as an auditor and become essentially a stay-at-home husband to help out with both the family and the professional side of the Meyer homestead. On a purely economic level, the decision seemed to make sense. Stephenie's income was more than sufficient to keep the family afloat. Stephenie has often indicated that making it possible for Christiaan to quit his job as an auditor and to go back to school full time was her present to him. Having her husband around did a lot for Stephenie on a personal level and it allowed Christiaan more quality time with the boys. And having now successfully dealt with his illness, it seemed that the time was right for a change of lifestyle for the family.

This is a subject that has been largely glossed over by the media and Stephenie has never really talked about it. There were those whispers that Christiaan's male ego might have been ruffled by his wife being the primary breadwinner in the family. But there seemed to be no problems in the decision. Suffice it to say, it all seemed to work.

Into April 2007, Summit Entertainment had moved ahead in active pre-production on the movie version of *Twilight*. The search had gone out for both a director and screenwriter to pilot the fortunes of what Summit hoped would be a film franchise that would rival the Harry Potter series. They did not have a hard-and-fast rule about who and what gender their choices would be. But after a thorough search and a lot of meetings, including a passing look from Harry Potter film director Christopher Columbus, who had to pass because he was working on another project, two women, director Catherine Hardwicke and screenwriter Melissa Rosenberg, were brought aboard the *Twilight* express.

Both choices seemed at odds with the preconceived notions of a writer and director on even a moderately budgeted big studio picture. Horror, the supernatural, and even a modicum of special effects were viewed as the area for male directors and writers. But there was that element of romance to contend with and so women in these pivotal positions seemed to make sense.

Hardwicke had made her reputation along the art house–Sundance circuit with well received but very small films like *Thirteen* and *Lords of Dogtown*. Rosenberg had more than a decade's worth of television writing credits, including *Ally McBeal*, *Hercules: The Legendary Journeys*, *The O.C.*, and *Dexter*, but had never earned a motion picture credit.

The luck of the draw, primarily from Stephenie's point of view, was that both Hardwicke and Rosenberg were immediately very sympathetic to the tale spun by Stephenie. Especially Hardwicke, a fan of the books, who expressed her initial feelings about making *Twilight* in an interview with *MediaBlvd*.

"The earlier script they had before was just pretty crazy," she declared. "This was not the girl from the book that I love. It wasn't like 'I wanted to do my own thing.' I wanted to do what Stephenie had created, and make it as cool, make everybody just embrace it and make those characters come to life."

Rosenberg began fashioning an outline for the *Twilight* script during the summer of 2007, exchanging ideas and notes with Hardwicke and, by association, keeping Stephenie well in the creative loop. The author, still the pessimist and smarting from the Paramount fiasco, found her early dealings with Hardwicke and Rosenberg to be surprisingly pleasant and, by Hollywood standards, straightforward, which instantly put the lie to the time-honored cliché that women, especially when it came to all things creative, could not get along.

Stephenie was particularly thrilled that in an industry notorious for taking source material and promptly discarding it, the filmmakers were legitimately interested in her ideas.

"I didn't go in thinking it had to be my way," she told www.about.com. "I really didn't want to step on anyone's toes. I didn't know how to make a movie and I didn't want to get in the way or screw it up somehow, so I let them come to me and they did."

The summer months turned out to be hectic on a number of fronts.

In preparation for the August 7, 2007, release of *Eclipse*, Stephenie's touring and book promotion schedule had switched to high gear. With Christiaan home, dutifully minding the boys, and assistants available to handle any business matters on the home front, Stephenie was logging major airline miles in such far-flung locations as London, Detroit, and her home base of Arizona.

Going to London for the first time was an eye-opening experience. She did manage some time to enjoy the sights and was amazed at the U.K. reception and how well this U.S.-based story had traveled across the pond. And she was somewhat but happily surprised when she found that often tough urban centers like Detroit had also found the heart in her books.

Back in Hollywood, things were no less hectic for Hardwicke and Rosenberg.

With the treatment for *Twilight* still rounding into shape, word came down that conflicts between the film studios and the Writer's Guild of America could force a strike on October 31, 2007. Consequently a completed *Twilight* script would have to be ready by that date to avoid a delay in production. Fortunately Hardwicke and Rosenberg had been in the moviemaking business long enough to experience the threat of work stoppage before and simply readjusted their deadlines to get *Twilight* done and to make it work.

Stephenie did not know about things like writer's strikes and, with her opinion of Hollywood still on the shaky side, news about the possible strike seemed to her like the proverbial other shoe about to drop. And so she was further amazed to constantly receive phone calls from Hardwicke, no matter where she was in the world, asking her what she thought about an element of the treatment or what her thoughts were in regards to something they were thinking. The best Stephenie could come up with in response to this unheard-of interest in what she had to say was . . .

"Really nice."

Little, Brown and Company were pulling out all the stops in marketing what they felt was their top priority of the 2007 book season. At what was described as an "Eclipse Prom," in which fans and the author showed up dressed for the prom, Stephenie read the first chapter of *Eclipse* to two sold-out crowds at Arizona State University. On the day of the reading, Little, Brown released a special edition of the previous novel, *New Moon*, that contained the first chapter of *Eclipse*. By this time, Stephenie had grown into the marketing side of things and helped things along by posting the first chapter of *Eclipse* on her own Web site. She also agreed to post "a quote a day" from the new novel in the thirty-seven days leading up to the official release date.

It is interesting to note that, by now, Stephenie had developed a real taste for getting the word out. And Little, Brown took great pains to keep her upbeat on the matter with imaginative twists on the typical author publicity tour. The "prom" was one such approach. So was a bookstore Web site video shot outdoors in which Stephenie, surrounded by a group of admiring fans, answered questions.

However, because she was now more business savvy, there were still those occasions when she would dig her heels in and the release of *Eclipse* would prove to be one of those moments. Stephenie was aware that J. K. Rowling's final Harry Potter novel, *Harry Potter and the Deathly Hallows*, was scheduled to come out right around the time of *Eclipse*. Stephenie told www.timesonline.com that she was not thrilled at the news.

"I pitched a fit with my publisher because I did not want my book to come out so close to hers. I saw a tidal wave of Harry Potter that would erase *Eclipse*. They said 'trust us.' I thought that the book would disappear."

Little, Brown was being very careful about not having the kind of leaks that plagued *New Moon* hinder *Eclipse*. Advance copies of the book, normally a solid publicity tool to drum up good word of mouth for an upcoming release, were not sent out. Into July, there had not been any leaks of plot particulars and the numerous fan Web sites, thanks in large part to personal requests by Stephenie, were being loyal and on their best behavior. *Eclipse* remained under a well-mannered but strict lockdown.

That is until July 25, 2007, when Barnes & Noble

The author, Stephenie
Meyer, in 2008.
(*©Summit
Entertainment/
Photofest*)

Robert Pattinson and Kristen Stewart on the set of the *Twilight* movie.
(*Maverick Films/The Kobal Collection*)

From left: director Catherine Hardwicke, actor Kristen Stewart, and writer Stephenie Meyer, on the set of *Twilight*, 2008. (*©Summit Entertainment/Courtesy Everett Collection*)

above: Members of the *Twilight* cast. Shown from left: Kellan Lutz, Nikki Reed, Elizabeth Reaser, Robert Pattinson, Peter Facinelli, Ashley Greene, and Jackson Rathbone. (*©Summit Entertainment/Photofest*)

right: A poster for the *Twilight* movie. (*©Summit Entertainment/Courtesy Everett Collection*)

Stephenie speaks and signs copies of her book *The Host* at the Mall of America in Bloomington, Minnesota, May 6, 2008. (*Tony Nelson/Retna*)

left: Stephenie Meyer speaks on stage at the Breaking Dawn Concert Series at the Nokia Theatre at Times Square on August 1, 2008 in New York City. (*Brad Barket /Getty Images*)

right: Stephenie poses for a portrait in Beverly Hills, California on Saturday, November 8, 2008. (*Associated Press/Matt Sayles*)

Stephenie and her husband, Christiaan, arrive at the Los Angeles premiere of *Twilight* at the Mann Village and Bruin Theaters on November 17, 2008 in Westwood, California. *(Steve Granitz / Getty Images)*

Stephenie signs autographs at the *Twilight* film premiere, Los Angeles, California, November 17, 2008. *(Rex USA)*

Robert Pattinson and Kristen Stewart at the *Twilight* film premiere, Los Angeles, California, November 17, 2008. (*Rex USA*)

above: Robert Pattinson greets his fans at the *Twilight* film premiere in Munich, Germany on December 6, 2008. (*Rex USA*)

left: Stephenie Meyer and Peter Facinelli, who plays Dr. Carlisle Cullen in the *Twilight* films, at Summit Entertainment's *Twilight* world premiere after party on November 17, 2008 in Westwood, California. (*Alexandra Wyman / Getty Images*)

left: A movie poster for *New Moon. From left:* Robert Pattinson, Taylor Lautner, and Kristen Stewart, 2009. (© *Summit Entertainment/ Courtesy Everett Collection*)

Twilight fans love to have their photo taken with "Bella's Truck", a 1952 Chevy pickup parked at the Forks Chamber of Commerce's Visitor Center in Forks, Washington. (*Chris Cook/ForksForum.com*)

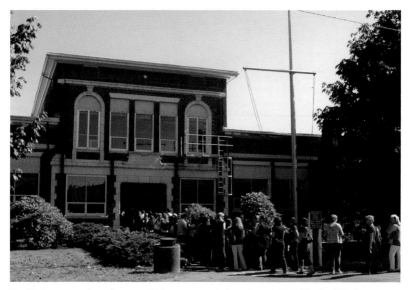

Twilighters gather for a walking tour of the circa 1925 Forks High School building during the Bella's Birthday–Stephenie Meyer Day celebration, September 13, 2008. *(Chris Cook/ForksForum.com)*

Forks Thriftway, the only large grocery store in Forks, is where Bella shops in the *Twilight* books. *(Chris Cook/ForksForum.com)*

A must-stop for visiting Twilight fans is the Forks High School Spartans sign. An exact copy of the sign appeared in the film version of the book *Twilight*. (*Chris Cook/ForksForum.com*)

About one thousand Twilight fans gathered at Tillicum Park in Forks during the Bella's Birthday–Stephenie Meyer Day celebration, September 13, 2008. (*Chris Cook/ForksForum.com*)

Booksellers accidentally shipped one thousand advance copies of *Eclipse* to customers who had preordered the book. Barnes & Noble apologized, citing a computer error as the cause for the early shipment. Computer error or not, the cat was out of the bag. Little, Brown and Stephenie moved swiftly to prevent any leaks.

The fan Web sites remained in lockstep, shutting down their operations at Little, Brown's request to prevent any spoilers from slipping out. In an open letter to the Web site Twilight Lexicon and other Web sites, Stephenie pleaded with those who had gotten advance copies of *Eclipse* not to reveal the ending until everybody had a chance to read and enjoy the book.

In an attempt to avoid further unpleasantness with a very important publisher, Barnes & Noble eventually tracked down seven hundred of the copies just as they were about to be loaded onto a UPS truck for delivery. Stephenie remained a good sport about the situation and praised the bookseller for its diligence in cleaning up the possible disaster. Amazingly, no leaks of the kind that marred *New Moon*'s release happened with *Eclipse*.

Well, almost no leaks.

Not too long before the official publication date, Stephenie loaned a relative a copy of the manuscript, assuming it was okay for the family to have a look as long as it went no further. When the relative asked if she could pass it along to another relative, Stephenie innocently said okay. Unfortunately, that person took it upon herself to pass it along to a third family member who, in turn, passed it along to her friend who, in turn, made copies for her friends.

Needless to say, Stephenie was extremely angry and upset when she found out *Eclipse* was slowly but surely getting out. Stephenie arranged a meeting with the people currently in possession of the copies and told them, in no uncertain terms, that she could not continue to write under the stress of her work getting out and if they told their friends anything about the book, she would stop writing forever. The threat, whether real or not, worked and they all kept silent until long after the official release date of *Eclipse*.

Stephenie was in a state of grace and fulfillment as she counted down the days and then the hours with her family. She was already well into the writing of *Breaking Dawn*, reportedly the final book in the romantic vampire series, and doing a final round of telephone interviews. However, much of her thoughts at the time were most certainly centered on the dream and the impact it had had on her life.

The dream had become a reality. But for Stephenie, the charm was that it was still a dream. A dream that had come true.

With the success of her books, Stephenie was now faced with other tasks connected to her creations. Despite the fact that *Twilight* had not even been made yet, Summit was anxious to have Stephenie sign on the dotted line for the company to do film versions of all the books. As always there was some trepidation, but being satisfied with the way things had been handled on the first film, she agreed.

Merchandising was a whole other matter.

Whenever a property became superpopular, it was inevitable that people would want to step in and license the title and the image for all manner of merchandise— from T-shirts to jewelry to posters . . . to who knows what. Stephenie took a decidedly hands-on approach to that area. She was not against the licensing per se. However, she was adamant that anything that went out under the *Twilight* brand be in good taste and in keeping with the tone of the books. Without going into too much detail, Stephenie waded through a literal mountain of proposals and ideas. Most of them she found not at all to her taste or liking. But a select few she did sign off on.

Eclipse was officially unveiled at the stroke of midnight on August 7, 2007. Confident that the book would do a massive amount of sales, Little, Brown printed one million copies of the first edition, ten times more than they had done for *New Moon*. Their confidence in the book was rewarded when *Eclipse* sold 150,000 copies within the first twenty-four hours of its release.

Observers of the book business were surprised at the quick ascendency of the Twilight series, a point driven dramtically home when *Eclipse* succeeded in knocking off the latest Harry Potter book from the number one slot on the *New York Times* Best Seller List, adding fuel to the fire that Stephenie had not only equaled but surpassed J. K. Rowling as the reigning queen of young adult literature. It was a comparison that Stephenie continued to take in stride but did not dwell on.

Reviewers continued to take occasional shots at Stephenie's writing style and storytelling structure but, as always, the critics largely weighed in on the upside. *People* magazine said, "The book has a hypnotic quality that puts the reader right inside the dense, rainy thickets of Forks." *Publishers Weekly* chimed in with "The legions of fans . . . will ecstatically devour this third installment." *Entertainment Weekly* bestowed the title on Stephenie as "the world's most popular vampire novelist since Anne Rice."

Stephenie marked the day with an appearance on the television show *Good Morning America*. And anyone who saw that interview had evidence to just how comfortable she was with that side of the writing life. There were still some butterflies, but gone were the days that she would throw up before an interview or event. Her responses were polished. She was patient with the questions she had heard so many times before. Stephenie came across as very grateful, very real, and very human. One thing was certain: Stephenie Meyer had kept her humanity through it all. She was still the housewife and mom whose dream had come true.

nine

Putting Her Foot Down

Melissa Rosenberg was working 24/7 to finish the *Twilight* script before October 31, 2007. And it was not an easy task.

Film adaptations of books are difficult at best and movie studios are always conscious of a film's running time and how many showings there are per screen per day. *Twilight* was turning out to be exhibit A for the reality of the business.

Much of *Twilight* the book had to be condensed to accommodate *Twilight* the movie's expected two-hour running time. Not surprisingly, some characters from the book did not appear in the screenplay. Scenes from the book were changed or eliminated. At Catherine Hardwicke's suggestion, a voice-over of Bella explaining her inner thoughts and guiding the proceedings was added. All of which was done in the name of keeping *Twilight*'s characters and story arc the same as the book.

And they were quick to run any of the changes and compromises by Stephenie for her blessing when they had to be made.

Stephenie recalled in a 2008 press junket for *Twilight* that she was happily kept in the loop from the first draft.

"They let me see the script and said, 'What are your thoughts?' I sent them back the script with red marks and it was always things like 'Wouldn't Bella say this more like this? Wouldn't this sound more like her voice?' It was never like 'This whole scene needs to go.' The script was in really good shape from the beginning. But they let me have input and they took 90 percent of what I said and just incorporated it right into the script."

Stephenie's involvement in the film version of *Twilight* was taking up a lot of her time and mental energy. And so it seemed at the time she was so preoccupied with the film that nobody would blame her if she took a hiatus from writing. She was also totally immersed in the continuation of the Twilight saga on a couple of very complex fronts.

Breaking Dawn, the fourth and final chapter in Edward and Bella's romance, was shaping up as a three-ring circus of storytelling in which, through Bella's voice, we deal with the possibility of her turning, marriage, and the complexities of childbirth. The second section of the book tells of Jacob's interest in the upcoming birth, the horrendous birth of the vampire daughter, and Bella's turning by Edward to save her life. The third section winds up the story and the saga with Bella learning to live the vampire life and the final expression of her forever-after romance with Edward.

Given the mammoth undertaking that *Breaking Dawn* had become, it was not surprising that Stephenie's musical choices for the Twilight series final act was equally big and ultimately broken down by sections of the book. Muse and Arcade Fire were well represented as her emotional guides. Others on the long list of good music included "White Wedding" by Billy Idol, "Congratulations" by Blue October, "Dark Blue" by Jack's Mannequin, and "Today" by Smashing Pumpkins.

Breaking Dawn had enough story for three books and it is a fair assessment that the notion of taking the last element of the Twilight story and spinning it off still further made some creative as well as economic sense. Stephenie's choice to wrap it up in one big package was a brave one, a challenging one and, perhaps, a sign that she was tired of the romantic vampire saga and wanted to put it to rest. At least for a while.

But if that was the case, her not-so-secret dalliance with *Midnight Sun*, the long talked about companion to *Twilight* told from Edward's point of view, would seem an odd choice. But maybe not so.

Through countless interviews, Stephenie has made it plain that she had a particular affinity for Edward and, if the series were truly poised to come to an end, giving Edward his voice would truly cement the relationship between Stephenie and her favorite character.

Needless to say, going into the later stages of 2007, Stephenie was playing fast and loose with her audience's expectations. How it would play out at that point was anybody's guess.

However, Stephenie, at some point in writing the final book, reinforced the long-held notion that, despite her feelings for Edward, the Twilight saga had always been about Bella. She had always felt that *Breaking Dawn* was the place for Bella's story to end and that the conclusion of the book was also the end of a coming of age odyssey for Bella.

Stephenie also used her Web site to address the feeling that she could have stretched out the Bella story line indefinitely. "I suppose I could try to prolong her story unnaturally, but that wouldn't be interesting enough to keep me writing."

Stephenie's feeling that *Breaking Dawn* had turned into a challenge not presented by the previous three books was proven shortly after she turned in the manuscript. The book was long, which, in and of itself, was not a surprise as the first three novels had all been in excess of four hundred pages.

But *Breaking Dawn* was huge by comparison and it was strongly suggested by her publisher that 20,000 words be cut. It was also once again suggested that Stephenie might want to seriously consider turning *Breaking Dawn* into two books. Stephenie agreed to cut a massive amount of text from the manuscript, but sided with her fans in not going in the direction of turning one book into two. She was concerned that her audience would have to wait a full year and have to buy another book to finally see the story through.

There were also suggestions from her editor and publisher that the sex and birth scenes were too realistic and that Stephenie might want to consider softening them. Stephenie momentarily put aside her aversion to graphic horror when she indicated that those scenes were quite naturally written and that they did not seem too graphic to her. But she did end up going back and cutting short some of the bloody and violent descriptions.

Meanwhile plans continued afoot for production to begin on *Twilight*. The studio budgeted the movie at $37 million, a rather modest amount by big studio film standards. A schedule of forty-four days was slotted to begin in early March and run through early May of 2008.

Reports from the the town of Forks indicated filmmakers were doing everything in their power to make sure that at least a portion of *Twilight* was actually filmed in that town.

In January 2008, Catherine Hardwicke flew up to Forks with the film's director of photography and a location scout and scouted out possible locations in and around First Beach for a pivotal sequence that would involve Edward and Bella. Prior to Hardwicke's visit, area location scouts had descended on the town, taking a lot of pictures of various locations, but showing particular interest in Forks High School.

Things were looking good for location shooting in Forks until money got in the way. The state of Washington refused to offer logistical and financial incentives necessary to make shooting in Forks feasible for the production company.

Although it was tempting to shoot even a small part of the film in the actual town of Forks, the state of Oregon ultimately came through with a more attractive support package, and so the decision was made that *Twilight* would be filmed in and around Portland and St. Helens, Oregon.

Casting began in earnest near the end of 2007. And it quickly became evident that few of the casting choices would go unchallenged in one way or another.

Kristen Stewart's selection for the role of Bella was actually the easiest. When the studio's choice to play Carlisle Cullen fell out of contention, Peter Facinelli, director Hardwicke's choice, replaced him. Likewise, the role of Emmett Cullen went to Kellan Lutz when the original actor for the role was not able to do the part.

Stephenie indirectly fed some controversy when it came to casting Ashley Greene in the role of Alice Cullen. Fan backlash against the choice of Greene centered on the fact that the actress was seven inches taller than the character was described in the book. Stephenie added fuel to the controversy when she told a reporter that she felt actress Rachael Leigh Cook most resembled her vision of Alice.

Stephenie's interest in the casting process was not something she took lightly. She had long indicated that even as she was writing *Twilight*, she always saw the story as a very visual experience and that she had mentally cast a movie version of the book many times before.

Eventually it came to the all-important casting of Edward. Robert Pattinson was among those who auditioned for the role. Despite his British good looks and a pedigree that included a role in another big budget fantasy series, Harry Potter, he was on the bubble when it came to the director's choice. But an impromptu audition between Pattinson and Stewart on the bed in Hardwicke's home decidedly tipped the balance in the young actor's favor.

However the young actor's candor would get him in no small measure of trouble shortly after his casting in the role. He admitted to not having read any of the books, which immediately drew the ire of Twilight fans who flooded the fan Web sites with rants that Pattinson should not be Edward and that a more appropriate choice should be made. The young actor pretty much made light of the furor over his casting.

However, Stephenie, who was finding out full well about the back-biting side of celebrity, was visibly upset and, yes, heartbroken at the attack on Pattinson. At one point, she actually called the actor up and apologized for the negative response. She was relieved to find out that Pattinson was taking it all in good-natured stride and was determined to prove his detractors wrong.

For her part, Stephenie was quite happy with the choice as she explained in several interviews including one with *MediaBlvd Magazine*. "Edward was really a hard one to cast. I didn't really know if there was anyone who could do it. I knew it was going to be a version of Edward, but I didn't know what it was going to be. When I found out that they had chosen Rob I looked him up and thought, 'Yeah, he's definitely got that vampire thing going on.'"

Once production actually began on *Twilight*, Stephenie made a point to fly up the Oregon locations to observe. Everything about the filmmaking process proved eye-opening. She was particularly delighted to watch scenes from the book unfold in real life with actors playing her fictional creations.

On one of those trips, she sat down with Pattinson and, during the course of their conversation, discovered her faith in him had been justified. He had ultimately gone on to read the first three novels and, in a bit of method acting, began to avoid his friends and acquaintances and to stay out of the sun in an attempt to develop the vampire look and attitude required for the role of Edward.

But that did not mean it was a total lovefest between the pair. Pattinson is an opinionated and self-assured actor. His approach to playing Edward was not exactly what Stephenie had in mind for her creation. There was a spirited give-and-take between the two that ultimately met somewhere in the middle and to everybody's satisfaction.

The scenes with Pattinson she had observed showed him to be the perfect fit for Edward. In fact, Stephenie was so impressed with his professionalism and dedication in the role that she decided to help the process along by letting Pattinson and director Hardwicke look at a few rough chapters of *Midnight Sun* to better help the actor and director get a handle on how they should be playing the film from Edward's perspective.

In hindsight, Stephenie would often have some second thoughts about letting anyone see even parts of that book in its raw form. The writing was nowhere near polished at that point and the story was not completely coherent. And not too far from the back of her mind was the fear that, like her previous books, this totally incomplete and unedited version of *Midnight Sun* might also leak out.

Throughout the course of filming, it had been suggested that Stephenie do a small cameo in a scene as kind of a present for her fans. Stephenie was reluctant at first, her shyness leaping to the fore. She was also concerned that it would be what she considered one of those dumb crowd scenes where she would walk through the camera frame and then out, a glorified extra.

But she finally relented and, on the day in question, Stephenie was escorted on to a diner set and positioned at the counter and good-naturedly advised by Hardwicke to be lost in thought as she crouches over the counter. The scene is essentially a transitional one in which Bella and Charlie are in deep conversation regarding the latest news about Waylon's murder. But as the camera pans, it suddenly comes to a stop and holds on Stephenie for a few beats before moving on. Just long enough for die-hard fans to realize that the author of *Twilight* was also in the movie. The consensus of those on the set was that Stephenie performed the handful of takes of the scene like a pro.

The willingness of the filmmakers to allow Stephenie to make suggestions at various points in the scripting, casting, and actual filmmaking process went largely without a hitch. In fact, the major bone of contention came during a rather sexually charged kiss between Edward and Bella. Stephenie offered that the kiss as filmed got in the way of the gradual evolution of their physical relationship in the other books and, subsequently, the movies. She was stalwart in saying that the kiss was now too much too soon and would throw other elements of their relationship out of balance. Hardwicke conceded the point and the kiss was toned down in a reshoot.

Stephenie has often looked back at those moments with some unease. She admits to having always been more critical of herself and has always been reluctant to step forward and be critical of others.

"But it's been good for me in general to speak up because I've been so invested in this," she explained in *Entertainment Weekly*. "I've forced myself to step forward and say 'I don't like this.' But I'm glad I did it and I don't think I stepped on too many toes."

Stephenie returned to Cave Creek and back into the whirl of media and promotion. Her days were filled with interviews and publicity events centered around both the movie and the upcoming *Breaking Dawn*. Nights were still taken up with writing, as was the tradition started by her father—reading bedtime stories to her children.

But one element of the bedtime stories was now inexorably altered. Her boys were now older and more prone to gossiping with their friends. When they were younger, Stephenie would often read them passages of her books. Now with the threat of leaks at every turn, she had decided that her books were off their reading list.

But that did not mean that word about *Breaking Dawn* was not getting out. The magazine *Entertainment Weekly* released an excerpt from the book on May 30. Stephenie reprieved her "quote of the day" on her Web site beginning July 12. The first chapter of *Breaking Dawn* was released as part of the special edition of *Eclipse*.

During the writing of *Breaking Dawn*, Stephenie had become attracted to the rock group Blue October and their music became an important element of her playlist that she listened to while writing the book. And so when it came time to do a series of four big city promotional events to coincide with a release of *Breaking Dawn*, Stephenie came up with the idea of turning the events into a real rock concert atmosphere by having Blue October member Justin Furstenfeld come along as her supporting act, performing a set of the band's music before Stephenie hit the stage. The events in New York, Chicago, Los Angeles, and Seattle all sold out within an hour of the tickets going on sale.

It proved to be a well-executed concept in which what could have been a rote and predictable exercise by now was amped up by the music that had guided her creatively. Stephenie basked in the high energy of those events and clapped along with the fans when the band performed. More and more, Stephenie was liking this world that could incorporate her two favorite loves, words and music.

Many bookstores jumped on the *Breaking Dawn* band-wagon, setting up midnight release parties for the book that saw thousands of fans lining up hours before the book officially went on sale. Little, Brown, confident that *Breaking Dawn* would continue its mass appeal, printed up a record 3.7 million first edition copies of the book.

And despite everybody's best efforts, some copies of the book were mistakenly released early to a grocery store in the small town of Eagle Pass, Texas, who had their copies on July 28.

At the stroke of midnight on August 2, 2008, the romantic saga of Edward and Bella officially came to an end, and 1.3 million copies of the book were sold within the first twenty-four hours. The book debuted on the *New York Times* Best Seller List.

As expected, fans loved it. Not so expected was that reviews of *Breaking Dawn* were, to a large extent, negative in tone.

Almost every element of the book, from story line to character development to the uncharacteristic childbirth sequence and a happy ending that to many reviewers seemed more of an afterthought, were put under a critical microscope. But there were just as many that found the charm in the final book.

Time magazine said, "A wild but satisfying finish to the ballad of Bella and Edward." The *Chicago Tribune* said, "Witty writing . . . a fun read." *School Library Journal* review called it, "Captivating."

Stephenie was upset at some of the nastier critiques of *Breaking Dawn* but, as with previous books, took the critical beating of *Breaking Dawn* in stride.

"There was going to be no way to please everyone," she said with a shrug during a *USA Today* interview. "That's always been a problem. But this is the ending I wanted all along. That's the important thing."

A minor flap occurred when stories began appearing that indicated that Stephenie had gone to the dark side in explaining the particulars of vampire sex that, admittedly, were a sudden jolt to readers who had come to expect a more gentle approach to the subject matter. Stephenie was upset at having been "misquoted," but stopped short of a complete clarification because she did not want to ruin that element of the story for the readers.

Sadly what should have been a moment of triumph as the series came to its conclusion was marred when the writer, Jordan Scott, of a barely heard of book called *The Nocturne* made a public demand that Stephenie and her publisher cease and desist from distributing *Breaking*

Dawn, claiming that it contained a story line taken from her book, which was published in 2006.

Scott claimed in stories published by both www.tmz.com and www.examiner.com that several scenes and actual bits of dialogue were taken directly from her book. Stephenie and Little, Brown announced that they had no knowledge of the writer or the book. The cease and desist order eventually went nowhere. Little, Brown assured Stephenie that these kinds of lawsuits come with the territory when a writer is immensely popular.

Stephenie did not take it seriously but, coming as it did at the end of a very long promotional tour and at what should have been a happy time, it all just seemed a bit tired, a bit confusing, and, yes, more than a little bit sad.

ten

The Midnight Hour

Even though *Breaking Dawn* was now officially out there, Stephenie was still on the road.

She attended an event in Seattle and some last-minute regional appearances in bookstores and local interview shows. But rather than hitting the wall of media exposure, Stephenie, in the face of the overwhelming interest, was calm, cool, and, dare we say it, collected.

Her smile seemed legitimate in the face of nonstop cameras and interviews. The enthusiasm she continued to express was contagious. Her belief in the worth of her creation and its offshoot was boundless.

The big reason for her relaxed state was the fact that, with *Breaking Dawn*, the romantic saga of Edward and Bella was over. But with the inevitable questions of what happens next, she was cagey in her responses. She was not shy about talking about her first what she considered adult novel, the science fiction romance *The Host,* which was nearing completion. However, when it came to the question of any further adventures of the vampire and human lovers, she danced around the notion of "never say never."

In a round-robin series of press junkets following the completion of principal photography on *Twilight* she told the likes of www.about.com and *Entertainment Weekly* that "It's done for now. I mean I can't promise that I won't get lonely for the Cullens and come back to them in ten years. But right now I feel really satisfied with where it is so I'm not planning on doing anything with it. But you know, no guarantees."

The "no guarantees" comment was more than just a sly tease. For as Stephenie finished up the press tour for *Breaking Dawn,* she knew full well that she already had one more bullet in her storytelling chamber.

Midnight Sun.

The origin of *Midnight Sun* goes back as early as 2006 when Stephenie was in the middle of a writing storm, literally jumping from *Eclipse* directly into *Breaking Dawn,* punctuated by equally long stints of editing. It was at that moment, brain totally frazzled by the tasks at hand, that Stephenie flashed upon the idea of rewriting *Twilight* totally from Edward's perspective.

The idea grew from thoughts into furtive notes and

fragments jotted down during trips to the post office and other routine chores. Eventually *Midnight Sun* became too much of an obsession to ignore and during a short span of time in which she could afford to absolutely put everything else aside, she wrote out a very rough draft of the first chapter. It was full of typos and all sorts of grammatical miscues, very much an unpolished bit of business. But that first chapter seemed to have the desired effect.

Stephenie put *Midnight Sun* aside and got down to writing for a living rather than for fun.

Truth be known, the days following the publication of *Breaking Dawn* were trying emotionally and mentally for Stephenie. She was burning the candle at every possible end. And any conversation with a family member or friend usually began with the phrase, "Don't you think you're working too hard?"

The reality was that she was, but eventually the obsession with getting Edward's side of the story out proved too much of a temptation and she sat down and wrote a very rough draft of *Midnight Sun*, twelve chapters, three hundred pages, and what she had determined as approximately half the length of a completed manuscript. She looked at what she had, promised herself that she would find the time to do a proper rewrite and edit, and then put it aside, only to leak copies on her own to a few trusted confidants, as well as Hardwicke and Pattinson on the set of *Twilight*.

Unfortunately, Stephenie's continued naïveté in the face of rampant technology was once again betrayed when, after returning home from the *Breaking Dawn* tour on August 28, 2008, she discovered that the very rough draft of the very incomplete *Midnight Sun* had been illegally posted on the Internet and subsequently freely distributed along the Web superhighway. Little, Brown was outraged at the blatantly illegal bit of thievery. For Stephenie, it was a little bit of anger and a whole lot of sadness.

Mentally she ticked off who had access to the manuscript. In the meantime, there was a lot of speculation about who could have done it. Some pointed to family members, citing what had happened with *Eclipse*. Others suggested that those in the *Twilight* cast and crew who had seen it had taken it upon themselves to post it. For her part, Stephenie reported that each of the copies of *Midnight Sun* she had handed out had specific changes she had made during different points on them. Consequently she was able to track down who she felt was the guilty party.

"The manuscript that was illegally distributed on the Internet was given to trusted individuals for a good purpose," she said in a prepared statement. "I have no comment beyond that and believe that there was no malicious intent meant with the initial distribution."

There were some other elements of that prepared statement that struck many who read it as harsh. One was that she was so upset about what had happened, if she were to attempt to write *Midnight Sun* right now, she would probably end up killing off all the characters.

Stephenie would later reveal that the statement was largely the work of lawyers with some of her own thoughts mixed in as well. She claims that in her original thoughts, the "kill everybody" statement was punctuated with a joke and no small amount of humor; but the intent and meaning were lost when mixed in with part of the cold, lawyerly sentiments.

But, at the end of the day, the experience had indeed left Stephenie a bit shell-shocked and uneasy. So much so that she announced in her statement that "My feeling is that I am too sad to continue working on *Midnight Sun* and so the book is on hold indefinitely."

While she did not show it outwardly, Stephenie was harboring a lot of resentment and sadness about what had happened. But she softened on the subject to eventually upload the twelve chapters of *Midnight Sun* onto her Web site for everybody to read, so those who had remained honest in regards to *Midnight Sun*'s illegal uploading could now see it for themselves, with the caution that it was nothing more than a rough work in progress.

Stephenie probably hoped that the whole topic of *Midnight Sun* would disappear, but she knew better. During the final press push for *Twilight* in the later part of 2008, the question was posed on a regular basis. And although still hurt by what had happened, her stance on the matter had softened.

To the point where she was now telling media outlets like *Entertainment Weekly* (and subsequently chronicled on www.wikipedia.com) that "My goal at this point is to go for two years without hearing the words *Midnight Sun*. And once I'm pretty sure that everybody has forgotten about it, I think I'll be able to get to the place where I'm alone with it again."

By the end of August 2008, Stephenie was in the closest she had been to a fragile place since she began writing *Twilight*. Juggling press requirements for both *Breaking Dawn* and the *Twilight* movie, continuing to deal with the never-ending parade of licensing and merchandising proposals and, yes, just trying to find the time to be a wife and mother, was a tiring experience.

And her current state was not going unnoticed by those closest to her. Family and friends began dropping not-too-subtle hints that she ought to just take some time off and do nothing. One of the most adamant in that regard was Stephenie's mother.

"The last twelve months have seemed like ten years," Stephenie confessed in a *People* interview. "My mother really worries [and she's always asking] 'Are you getting enough rest?' "

When she first began her writing career, she was more than happy to talk to anybody who had an interest. But now, with an army of publicists running interference, she was being more selective in what interviews she would do and how much of her time would be available. There were those days when it all began to seem like too much work.

Which is why on those days she would think back a scant month, to the last fun time she had before things got heavy—the 2008 San Diego Comic-Con.

This annual July gathering of the comic book and movie elite and just plain fans and geeks seemed to hold no pressure. She would be part of a panel, with the director and actors, trumpeting the upcoming release of *Twilight*. She would answer a few questions, many for the umpteenth time, sign a lot of autographs, and have the time of her life walking the aisles of an event steeped in fantasy and watching young and old alike dress up as their favorite comic book heroes and villains.

"I'm not afraid of being here," she happily told Reelz-Channel shortly after appearing before thousands at the *Twilight* panel. "I know my fans. They're cool people."

But just as quickly, it was back to the present and the countdown to the premiere of *Twilight*.

Stephenie had heard all the stories about authors experiencing the excitement and emotion of having their books turned into movies. Now she knew what it was all about because she was all of those things times ten.

Including, in the days leading up to the premiere, the fear that, despite having seen a rough cut of the film months earlier, something would go terribly wrong and the picture would be a disappointment.

The excitement continued to grow as she got on a plane to fly to Los Angeles for the November 17, 2008, premiere of *Twilight* in Westwood, California. Stephenie was enraptured by the Hollywood pomp of the evening. The red carpet. The paparazzi snapping pictures. The quick bits of interview that would make the eleven o'clock news. The after-party where she would mingle with the stars of the film and other celebrities.

Stephenie offered brave and hopeful sound bites to television and Web site interviewers on the way into the theater.

"I think they did a very good job of translating the book into the movie," she said on www.twilightlexicon. com as fans screamed out at her appearance. "You couldn't do it exactly the way the book was but it is a very good translation."

She remained hopeful inside the theater as the lights

went down. Two hours later all she could feel was that if she had *Twilight* on a loop, she probably would have watched it over and over all night.

From Stephenie's mouth to the filmgoing audience's ears.

Twilight grossed more than $7 million from only four midnight screenings on November 21, 2008. It grossed $36 million on its opening day, effectively covering the entire budget of the film. For its opening weekend in just the United States and Canada, *Twilight* took in $70 million. As of April 23, 2009, *Twilight* had brought in $380 million in worldwide ticket sales.

Much as they had been for the book, reviews of *Twilight* were decidedly mixed. Many pointed out an inherent silliness in the story line and concept. However, even those hard-nosed critics had to agree that, as an almost literary interpretation of young love, the movie would easily survive to become a pop culture classic.

The *Los Angeles Times* greeted the film's opening with "*Twilight* is unabashedly a romance. Maybe it is possible to be thirteen and female for a few hours after all." *USA Today* was less kind in its assessment when it said, "The novel was substantially more absorbing than the unintentionally funny and quickly forgettable film." *New York Press* said the movie was "A genuine pop classic that turns Meyer's book series into a Brontësque vision."

Needless to say, Summit Entertainment quickly

confirmed on November 22, 2008, that the wheels were already in motion to make a film version of *New Moon* a reality. And very soon.

Many speculated that Stephenie was quickly inching up to challenge J. K. Rowling as not only the most influential young adult writer in the world, but also the most profitable. Given the never-ending royalties, the money from the films and the mechandising, it was a safe bet that at the ripe old age of thirty-five, Stephenie Meyer would never have to work again.

Stephenie laughed at the notion that she never had to write another word. She was a writer.

Which meant there would always be a next word.

eleven

Next Word

Stephenie Meyer does sleep. At least that's the rumor.

However, going into 2008, her almost legendary prolific nature had reached almost mythic proportions. Four books in excess of six hundred pages each, more promotional air miles than any five authors put together. She had her family time, her church time. And she had ideas. . . .

Always new ideas.

Since the release of *Twilight*, Stephenie has always been quick with the tease of a new idea for a book or a new story that had taken up permanent residence in her head and would not go away. However, most media types took such comments as merely setups for what would happen after the conclusion of the four-book Twilight saga. Nobody in their wildest imagination ever considered that the author would actually kick-start other projects right in the middle of actively working to wrap up that series.

But then nobody really knew Stephenie Meyer.

If they did, they would have sensed that Stephenie was not a writer to rest on her laurels or ride one idea into the ground. There was also the sense of a "coming-of-age" as a writer with the conclusion of the Twilight series. Mentally she had long been chafing at the bit of doing something else and taking her talents in another direction.

During late 2006 and into 2007, Stephenie was in the typical eye of the hurricane. She was attempting to edit *Eclipse* while dealing with the early rush of obligations surrounding the *Twilight* movie. Taking a few precious days off to visit family in Salt Lake City, she was driving an endless, isolated highway. It was a rough ride. Music, even her favorite band Muse, would only take her so far. Her three boys had long since gotten tired of talking and were in the back watching movies. Boredom was setting in at a faster pace than the miles were clicking by. Stephenie often recalled the experience as driving through ugliness and desert.

"It's a drive I've made many times," she said in a www.bookreporter.com interview, "and one of the ways I keep from going insane is by telling myself stories."

On this particular drive, Stephenie came up with a whopper of a tale.

Before she knew it, Stephenie was imagining a science fiction–fantasy scenario in which a body-snatching alien inside the body of an earth girl has fallen in love with the earth girl's boyfriend, even as the earth girl attempts to block the alien's attempt at seducing the boyfriend. Instantly she realized what was happening—she had mentally begun to form an entire story.

"I could tell there was something compelling in the idea of such a complicated triangle," she told www.bookreporter.com. "I started writing the outline in a notebook and then fleshed it out as soon as I got to a computer."

Stephenie recalled in a www.sheknows.com interview that she felt driven to escape into something different.

"I knew this was something I needed to work on. I was having a hard time being away from the writing. I was editing at the time and that is a very different process. You don't get the same creative outlet from it at all. I needed something."

The basic premise of *The Host* was, in some ways, similar to the conception of *Twilight*. *Twilight* postulated that yes, there are vampires and then basically went on into the romantic and character-driven elements of the story. With *The Host* we are quickly through the successful alien invasion of earth and focusing on how the two factions learn to live with each other's strengths and frailties. The aliens are not truly evil. Neither are the vampires. And like *Twilight*, *The Host* focuses on the struggles of love and identity.

Similar to her feelings about *Twilight*, Stephenie never really saw *The Host* as being science fiction and so, although she has often likened her novel to that classic science fiction tale *Invasion of the Body Snatchers*, she was able to forgo the research into the genre and rough patches of hard science much as she had avoided all things horror and vampires with *Twilight*.

The reason being that *The Host*, much like all her other work, is about bigger truths: in this case the reality of what it means to be human in all of its physical and emotional shades.

But early on in the process, Stephenie maintained that while *Twilight* was about romance, *The Host* was about love with a big, somewhat grown-up capital L, love that Stephenie, always looking at the bigger picture, has often described as universal love.

It was kind of an unusual time to be starting what could easily turn into another literary franchise and a bit of a gamble. Stephenie was putting her efforts into editing *Eclipse* and also had the not too considerable pressure of ultimately turning *Breaking Dawn* into a final satisfying chapter. It was a book that was still at a fun stage.

And although her feelings were very good about

Little, Brown and Company, her contract with them did not extend beyond the end of the Twilight series. So, if she was so inclined, *The Host* could very easily put her in the uncomfortable position of turning on Little, Brown.

Stephenie completed *The Host* midway through 2007 and, while continuing to write and promote the Twilight books, quietly began putting *The Host* out to gauge interest from other publishers.

"There were several publishers interested in *The Host*," she said candidly in a 2008 interview with www. allthingsgirl.net. "I spoke with editors at many publishing houses to get a sense of how they would handle the property. I have to be honest, aspects of several houses tempted me."

But ultimately her loyalty to Little, Brown and the way they had marketed her and her books to the top of the bestseller lists tipped the scales. She signed a publishing deal for *The Host* with Little, Brown and Company at an extremely generous advance.

On the surface, Little, Brown and Company snatching up anything offered by Stephenie would seem to be an easy decision. She was a name and a brand that had sold millions for them. How could *The Host* be any less successful for them?

However, *The Host* was not going to be one of those books that they could easily drop into the young adult niche. The book, by Stephenie's own admission, was a bit more adult in content than the Twilight series had been. And while some of the elements of budding romance and choice that populated her vampire books were evidenced in *The Host,* they were wrapped up in what could be an off-putting science fiction package. So although the publishing house put the best possible face on it, they had to be holding their breath when *The Host* was released in May 2008.

Stephenie told www.sheknows.com that she was also on edge as she awaited the reception for *The Host.*

"Whenever I have a book come out, I tend to get really nervous. You might love it but someone else might hate it. With *The Host* it was a bit different. I was doing something that, in so many ways, was so completely different from what my fans, who love specific characters, are about."

Stephenie need not have worried.

The Host, released through Little, Brown's adult division, debuted at number one on the *New York Times* Best Seller List and would remain on the list for twenty-six weeks. Not surprisingly, the reviews were once again mixed but generous in their praise for Stephenie's attempt, conscious or otherwise, to prove that she could do other things.

The *Pittsburgh Post-Gazette* described the book as "A brilliant and fascinating premise. Its mixture of adventure and new love is just right to get lost in this summer." *USA Today* called it "An epic story of love, family and loyalty." *Library Journal* offered that "*The Host* lives up to the hype, blending science fiction and romance in a way that has never worked so well."

Despite the good reviews, Stephenie insisted in an Associated Press interview that the fans would ultimately tell her how successful *The Host* would be. "It would be cool if my existing fans liked it. And I hope to get some new readers who would never have gone to the young adult shelves."

The Host had originally been designed as a standalone book with no further adventures to follow.

But, as with the follow-ups to Twilight, Stephenie had grown to like the potential of the characters in *The Host* and, by March 2008, had announced that she was almost done with a sequel to the book with a tentative title of *The Soul,* and that she was now thinking in terms of a third book in the series to be entitled *The Seeker.*

While Stephenie has never looked at writing as a chore, by the time *The Host* was released, she was mentally very tired. Not tired enough to avoid doing the thing she loved to do, but tired of doing everything publicly that had become a part of the job description.

Make no mistake, Stephenie had evolved into the ideal spokesperson for her work and all its permutations. But now there was a yearning to just be by herself for a while, be with her family, read a bunch of books, and listen to a lot of music.

Of the latter, the group Jack's Mannequin had become a regular on her iPod listening list. Best described as a "piano-rock" band, Jack's Mannequin, and in particular singer-songwriter Andrew McMahon, had gained a significant following in the alternative music world and, given that pedigree, their insightful and philosophical lyrics set to a movable beat, had put them right in Stephenie's wheelhouse. And when Stephenie likes something, she tends to spread the good word around. So, early in 2008, it came to McMahon's attention that the band had a big supporter in Stephenie.

The singer-songwriter, like Stephenie a true freethinker, was flattered at the compliments she was paying them, especially when she made it clear that the band's music had influenced much of her recent work. But McMahon did not think too much more about it until some months later when the band was going through the annual sifting of video treatment ideas and possible video directors for the song "The Resolution" from their forthcoming album, *The Glass Passenger*. The process was dragging on, threatening to become too much like work.

Then one day, McMahon had an idea.

"I was talking to someone at our label," he said in an

MTV.com interview, "and said 'Let's try to do something different.'"

Different to McMahon meant contacting Stephenie with the invitation to not only create a concept for the video, but to direct it as well.

Stephenie jumped at the chance. It was something low-key. It was something new to challenge her creatively. And she was not going to let the fact that she knew nothing about directing get in the way.

"I'm just doing it because it's fun and it's an experience I never had," she related to MTV.com. "I didn't want to turn it down."

Stephenie began immersing herself in the song and its lyrics and came away with the notion of a fantasy fable set in the world of relationships gone awry and whether one can truly be finished with them. In Stephenie's mind, the story revolved around McMahon at his piano on a truck driving away from the encroaching sea and the siren call of a mermaid wanting him back. Eventually the temptation proves too great and he returns to the mermaid. The story, as envisioned by Stephenie, was rife with nuances and subtleties and interpreting it all would be dinner conversation for some time to come.

Creating the treatment was the easy part. Directing her vision? Well, that would be a whole different story.

Stephenie prepared for her directing debut by a

marathon viewing session in which videos by OK Go, Brand New, and My Chemical Romance played out in a seeming continuous loop. Stephenie was making mental notes regarding style and how things tended to work visually.

She felt she was ready.

What she had not counted on was the dollars and cents side of video making. Although they were a band definitely on the rise, Jack's Mannequin's budget for "The Resolution" was spartan and had to be shot in one day. Fortunately Stephenie and the band caught a break when they found an isolated stretch of Malibu, California, beachfront that contained every element of the video they would need in a matter of a few hundred yards.

On the day of the shoot, Stephenie, beneath a hot summer sun, was very workmanlike in setting up and shooting the three main set pieces that would make up the video. In conjunction with a veteran cameraman, Stephenie, feeling more a creative consultant than an actual director, patiently guided the pieces together.

The finished video, which was released on September 30, 2008, was a solid reflection of Stephenie's fantasy influence and attitude. There was a soft, almost gauzelike feel to the video, indicative of the isolation and emotional turmoil involved in the song. The dramatic moments were quiet. The cinema of it all was subtle and clipped, but no less effective.

It was a solid effort.

One that allowed Stephenie to take a break from the nonstop nature of her life that was lurking on the horizon.

twelve

Show Me the Money

Stephenie insisted to all who asked that 2009 was going to be a low-profile year for her.

She was cutting back on just about all her public appearances; she would do her part to promote the *New Moon* movie that was getting ready to go into production and that was about all. All of which did nothing to stop uncounted rumors and speculation from swirling around her.

One rumor that was not long in coming was that Stephenie was not well. She was quick to dismiss that one. She was a bit tired from all her nonwriting duties of the past three years but she was quite healthy. An official statement in that regard said, "Stephenie is currently focusing on being a writer."

That, in turn, led to the story emerging that Stephenie had finally gotten over being mad about the *Midnight*

Sun leak and was finally working on that book. Quick as a bunny came another response from her publisher that read, "Nothing has changed. Stephenie has no plans to move forward with *Midnight Sun* at this time. Stephenie is working on something else at the moment but she hasn't announced it yet. It is not Twilight related. When she's ready to reveal it, she will."

Stephenie's worldwide success was not without its detractors. Though her books had risen to become some of the biggest sellers on the planet, even the kinder critics would often take snide shots at her writing style as they were praising her storytelling skills. But it remained for famed horror writer Stephen King to fire the first dismissive shot at Meyer from another author during a February 2009 interview with *USA Today*.

"Meyer can't write worth a darn," King said in the interview. "She's not very good."

King went on to say that Stephenie's storytelling style was "exciting and it's thrilling but it's not particularly threatening because the characters are not overtly sexual."

Stephenie's fans took immediate offense and blasted King for his attacks on numerous fan sites. Stephenie took the high road and, to this point, has refused to make a comment.

Unfortunately, this would not be the last bit of discomfort Stephenie would experience in 2009. In April a woman named Heidi Stanton, who claimed to be a roommate of Stephenie's during her days at Brigham Young University, came forth with a lawsuit, claiming that Stephenie had stolen the idea for *Twilight* from a short story she had written during her college days. She further said that a professor at Brigham Young named Peter Benton had publically supported her claims.

Needless to say, the scoop-happy media was all over the story for a number of days. Stephenie was distressed and a bit amused at the claim. She eventually came out on her Web site to categorically deny that she ever had a roommate named Heidi, that there was not a professor at Brigham Young named Peter Benton, and that she has explained countless times how she came up with the idea of *Twilight*. She also chided the media for being quick to run with a story without checking the facts and warned her supporters not to believe everything they read.

As often happens in these cases, a lawsuit was never filed or pursued, and Heidi and her claims eventually went away.

Through the early months of 2009, it became an almost daily ritual for fans to check Little, Brown and Company and other Web sites for any news of upcoming books. But while the reports consistently were that Stephenie was working on something, there were no new books on the horizon. It had long been noted that

Stephenie was nearly finished with the follow-up to *The Host* well before that book came out, but it did not appear anywhere on the publishing schedule of Little, Brown.

Not that Stephenie needed to be in any hurry to get another book out. Her current catalogue was continuing to do quite well. In 2008 alone, Stephenie sold an estimated twenty-nine million copies of her books. And into 2009 that sales rate was showing no signs of letting up. It was reported that, in the first three months of 2009, 16 percent of all books sold were Stephenie Meyer titles. That works out to one in every seven books sold.

And Little, Brown was not going to let the fact that there was not a new Stephenie book get in the way of selling a wide array of Twilight book tie-ins and companion books that Stephenie did not write.

In March 2009, *Twilight Director's Notebook* hit the shelves; it was a large picture-filled diary in which director Catherine Hardwicke documented the ins and outs of making the film. But looking to flood the market throughout the remainder of the year and, in particular, to have the shelves stocked with new product to coincide with the release of the film version of *New Moon*, the titles just kept on coming.

These included *The Breaking Dawn Special Edition* on August 4, *The Twilight Journals* on October 13; *New*

Moon: The Complete Illustrated Movie Companion on October 6, *New Moon* trade and mass market movie tie-in books in September and October; and the *New Moon Collector's Edition* on October 6.

However, the potential pick of the lot was easily a book that Stephenie actually did write, *The Twilight Saga: The Official Guide*, a massive hardcover collection of character profiles, maps, cross-references, and genealogical elements relating to the four books of the Twilight odyssey. Stephenie had completed the book in 2008 in time for a proposed December 30 release date, but Little, Brown postponed that release to an as yet unannounced 2009 date to give the author and publishing house the time to add certain artistic elements to the book.

It seemed almost inevitable that with all the offshoots of Stephenie's creation, it would only be a matter of time when comic books would take their moment in the Twilight universe. So it was not that much of a surprise when, in July, two different comic book projects were announced.

The first came when Yen Press announced that it had entered into a deal with Stephenie and Little, Brown to do a Twilight graphic novel. The book, which would be drawn by Young Kim, would be in a stark manga style. Stephenie was given approval rights on each panel and she was impressed at the look and seemed happy that the graphic novel would add a progressive, artistic perspective to her story.

Also, at the 2009 San Diego Comic-Con, it was announced that Bluewater Productions, who had successfully published a bio-comic series called Female Force, which had profiled such female personalities as Michelle Obama and Oprah Winfrey, would publish a book on the life of Stephenie Meyer and her creation. This being comics, everybody seemed excited when Bluewater reported that the book would have a definite otherworldly feel and that Stephenie, in this world, would be more of a protagonist. The book, written by Ryan Burton with art by Dave MacNeil and Vinnie Tartamella, would come in two formats: one a standard twenty-two-page comic book and the other a double-sized collector's edition with such extras as the history of Forks.

Stephenie was not naïve about the fact that her creation had become a cottage industry with a license to print money. But she seemed to take a pragmatic attitude toward it. If it enhanced her creation in some way, she seemed okay with the literal sea of books coming out. If it was something her fans would appreciate, she was all for it. If it was something that would, financially, make her family's life more comfortable . . . well, you get the picture. Stephenie was cashing in, but in such a Stephenie kind of way, who could blame her.

That Stephenie's tales of vampire love were having a

worldwide impact on media and pop culture became evident in 2009 when The CW announced that *Vampire Diaries* would be in their fall television lineup. While based on the novels of L. J. Smith, one need not look too far into the series pilot story line to see that *Vampire Diaries* has borrowed quite a bit in terms of story, tone, and imagery from the Twilight series (despite the fact that the books were reportedly published before *Twilight*), which does not mean that ultimately *Vampire Diaries* will be a dud. But you know what they say about the sincerest form of flattery.

During the summer of 2009, Stephenie and her perceived target audience clicked in a big way when *Twilight* captured top honors in five categories at the MTV Movie Awards. The movie took home first place for Best Movie, Best Female Performance, Best Fight, Best Kiss, and Best Male Breakthrough Performance.

By the summer of 2009, Stephenie's low profile had pretty much come to an end. There was a *New Moon* on the horizon and it was time for her to get out there and let people know about it.

thirteen

New Moon *on the Rise*

Stephenie had heard stories about how fast Hollywood moved when it felt it had a moneymaking hot project on its hands. But the haste with which Summit Entertainment was moving on adapting the remainder of her Twilight saga to film even had the normally unflappable Stephenie scratching her head.

Because the hunt for the director for the film version of *Eclipse* was already on and close to completion, Summit had made the hunt for the new director a fairly stealthy operation with a fairly short list of candidates. At one point both *Variety* and United Press International broke what they thought was a major scoop when they announced that Juan Antonio Bayona, a veteran of Spanish cinema whose film *The Orphanage* had made a moderate splash in the United States, had been named by the company to direct *Eclipse*. If true, negotiations must have broken down because ultimately the film company had another idea.

Less than a month after production began on *New Moon*, Summit announced that David Slade, known in vampire circles for his film adaptation of the comic book *30 Days of Night*, had been selected to direct the movie version of *Eclipse*. They went on to proclaim that this third film would be in theaters during the summer of 2010, less than a year after the release of *New Moon*.

In subsequent weeks, there would be a seemingly endless stream of press announcements revealing actors signed on for the third picture and at least one quote from a Summit Entertainment rep—who requested anonymity—indicating that the company was already racing forward with plans for *Breaking Dawn* and that the film would be PG-13 despite the handful of graphic scenes in the book.

What caught one's eye in the initial announcement was a quote from Stephenie that said, "I am thrilled that David Slade will be directing *Eclipse*. He's a visionary filmmaker who has much to offer the franchise."

What seemed odd in this statement was the fact that Stephenie was indicating a familiarity with his work that she may not have had unless she had summoned up the courage to see *30 Days of Night* (his most well-known film), which runs contrary to her long-espoused aversion to graphic horror films. This seeming contradiction aside, Stephenie was once again proving to be a good soldier when it came to furthering the cause of her works.

However, by the time Slade was announced, Stephenie was already getting used to the idea that Summit moved in very unexpected ways.

On November 22, 2008, a mere three weeks after the company had announced that they had purchased the rights to the remaining three films, *Twilight* screenwriter Melissa Rosenberg was already hard at work on the script for *New Moon*. The Monday after *Twilight*'s opening weekend, Rosenberg handed in the completed draft of the script to Summit.

Shortly after that Summit announced that it was going ahead with *New Moon* with no director attached. Stephenie was concerned and more than a bit upset at the news. So were fans of the first film who were naïve to the fact that it was rare that a successful film franchise used the same director on every film. However, the question persisted: What had happened to Catherine Hardwicke?

The popular press played up "a difference in direction" and "scheduling problems." The reality, chronicled in the more business-oriented trades like *Variety*, painted a much deeper picture of the reason for the decision.

The reality was that Hardwicke and Summit remained in negotiation for two more weeks before she officially dropped out of the project. One of the main causes for the split was that *New Moon* was going to require a substantial amount of visual effects work and, consequently, a much longer prep time than Summit was willing to give Hardwicke. Another stumbling block was that a literal adaptation of *New Moon* would have required Edward to be absent from much of the film and Summit did not want their reigning sex symbol in a limited role. Rosenberg's initial draft of the script had figured out a way to get around that problem, but Hardwicke felt that script still needed many months of development while Summit wanted the movie in production immediately.

So at the end of the day, Hardwicke walked.

While Stephenie agreed with Summit's decision, she made it plain in a story that appeared in www.aceshow biz.com as well as on her own personal Web site that she had mixed emotions about the situation.

"I'm sad that Catherine is not continuing on with us for *New Moon*," she declared in early December 2008. "I'm going to miss her, not just as a brilliant director, but also as a friend."

Stephenie was getting a firsthand lesson in how Hollywood operated. But working seemingly to her advantage was her complete trust in those who worked for her and with her. She was still cautious in offering up opinions and statements in areas she did not feel qualified in despite the good working relationship she had with Summit to that point. Like a lot of writers, perhaps, she just wanted to be left alone to write and had a kind of tunnel vision on a lot of things that did not have anything to do with her writing process.

However, as offered in a *Los Angeles Times* interview, she was comfortable enough with the way Hollywood operated that she hoped she would be allowed to stay in the loop as movie versions of her work continued to unfold.

"I think I'd like to be more involved," she explained. "I feel like I had a really great level of involvement here. I've really enjoyed the people I've worked with and I just like hanging out with them. I'm so fascinated with how it all works."

On December 13, 2008 it was announced that director Chris Weitz had been chosen to direct *New Moon*. Weitz, who had built a substantial résumé on the strength of such films as the raucous teen comedy *American Pie* and the fantasy *The Golden Compass*, met with Stephenie shortly after the announcement and she came away from that meeting feeling positive about the choice.

"I can tell you he is excited by the story and eager to keep the movie as close to the book as possible," she said on www.aceshowbiz.com. "I'm really looking forward to seeing his vision for *New Moon*."

While it is a safe bet that Stephenie has never seen

American Pie, she had, in fact, seen *The Golden Compass* and had been quite taken with the way the director had turned big studio attitudes and modern technology into a delightful movie experience.

Unfortunately, hard-core fans were not as enthused with the change of director and were soon deluging the Internet with concerns about Weitz taking over the director's chair and what that meant for the possibility of a faithful adaptation of *New Moon*. To head off the bad vibe brewing, Weitz was pushed into the breach with a letter stating that he was devoting himself to making the very best and most faithful version of *New Moon* that could be brought to the screen.

Stephenie was once again brought in to smooth the fan's ruffled feathers when she went on her own Web site to assure her fans, "He [Weitz] is very aware of you, the fans, and wants to keep you all extremely happy. Torches and pitchforks are not going to be necessary."

But while Stephenie did her best to reassure the fans, Weitz seemed intent on continuing to antagonize them. Shortly after being named director, he said he was considering replacing actor Taylor Lautner, who portrayed Jacob Black in the first film, with a physically bigger actor to more accurately play the character in the sequel.

Again there were more howls of protest. However, Lautner wanted to keep the role badly enough that he immediately jumped into an extreme period of weight training and, in a month, put on thirty pounds of muscle. Weitz was impressed and Lautner was allowed to keep his job.

Meanwhile back at Forks, the failure of the state of Washington to come up with a suitable financial support package to lure the *Twilight* production to the state and, in particular, the town of Forks, had gone from a minor grumble to a major uproar. At a time when the economy in the state, and in small towns like Forks in particular, was bad, it seemed an outrage that the state could not make it comfortable for film companies to shoot there.

When it became known that *New Moon* would be shooting in Vancouver and Italy, it seemed to be the emphasis to push through favorable legislation for future productions. Such a bill was brought before the governor in early 2009 and was quickly signed.

In a 2009 interview with the local newspaper, the *Forks Forum*, Washington Film Works director Amy Dee hinted at things to come: "Since the governor signed the bill, our office has been flooded with calls from filmmakers and production companies from around the world. That said, my first call after I found out the bill had been signed was to Summit Entertainment to talk to them about the *Twilight* sequels."

New Moon began filming in late March 2009 in

Vancouver and wrapped up filming in Italy in late May. By all reports, things went surprisingly smoothly. Weitz, with his background in special effects movies, was more than capable of capturing the pivotal werewolf sequences. The returning actors from *Twilight* settled easily into their now familiar roles and meshed easily with the new actors and characters. Conspicuous by her absence from the set, at least initially, was Stephenie.

The reasons for that are many and valid. Although she was doing the occasional interview and charity event, Stephenie was being true to her word that she wanted to use this downtime to be with her family and write.

"It's hard for me to find time for everything," Stephenie told www.allthingsgirl.com in a 2008 interview. "It's a balancing act and I don't always do it perfectly. I make a conscious effort to spend time with my kids after school and to read to them at bedtime. My friends totally understand and they welcome me with open arms whenever I finally stagger out of my hole to be with them."

What she was writing "in the hole" at the time was a big part of the Internet chatter among her fans. She had long hinted that there might be a ghost story, with the working title of *Summer House*, or a time travel story in her future. And, in the wake of her Jack's Mannequin directing experience, she told a *Los Angeles Times* reporter that there could possibly be a book about a mermaid in her future. There was also the reported next book in *The Host* trilogy. Stephenie had indicated that there had been interest in a movie version of *The Host* and some were of the opinion she had to make herself available for talks and a possible deal on that front.

There was also the sudden rush of business trend stories that may have persuaded Stephenie that it was time to go below the radar for a while.

First came the latest series of articles proclaiming that, indeed, Stephenie was the new J. K. Rowling, complete with sales figures to prove it. But there were also the stories about booksellers being alarmed that sales might now suddenly drop off now that the final book in the Twilight series was completed and whether, by association, anything Stephenie did that was not vampire-related would ever match that series. It had to be hard for Stephenie to concentrate on writing when her future, and a not necessarily upbeat future at that, was already being bandied about in the press.

It would not have been too much of a leap for the author to pop up to Vancouver for a quick look at *New Moon*, but the consensus, at least by those who would regularly see her around Cave Creek during this period, was that she was having too much fun just being a wife and mother to even spend a day on a movie set.

But Stephenie's curiosity finally did get the better of her and, in early April, she did manage a quick jaunt to the Vancouver set where she watched the movie being shot, posed for some pictures, and gave some enterprising fans who managed to avoid the set's stringent security practices the shock of their lives when they spotted her walking around.

Word through the grapevine was that Stephenie's trip to Vancouver was twofold—to meet and greet and to film a cameo in *New Moon*. But if that had been Stephenie's intention, she came away sadly disappointed because no cameo was in the works for her in *New Moon*.

It had been a given in Twilight fandom that Stephenie would somehow wind up in the new movie, even if for a second. But as the days and weeks came and went during production and there was no news of Stephenie being in a scene, disappointment grew that *New Moon* would not contain an author appearance. That disappointment became more passionate when Weitz, not long after wrapping filming, conceded a blunder on that front in an interview with *Time*.

"But now I feel bad about it—as though I intended not to. But I had kind of forgotten that she had a cameo in the first one, and she never asked, she's very quiet and gracious about it. I don't know if she wanted to or not. I probably should have."

Weitz continued what appeared to be his propensity for not quitting while he was ahead when he told an MTV interviewer around the same time, "I think she

(Stephenie) may have decided against experiencing that whole thing again. People don't realize the sheer tedium a film set embodies. She was probably like, 'Well, I'll sit this one out.'"

Perhaps sensing that he might be muddying the waters, Weitz, in the same *Time* interview, acknowledged his intention to do right by Stephenie and the fans: "But Summit understands that it is Stephenie Meyer's world and really it's about recreating the experience the reader has, in some kind of faithful manner. Creating a picture that doesn't violate too badly the picture they [the fans] have in their minds."

And it was a growing concern that the Twilight fans might be getting too possessive and demanding of their favorite books and how they are portrayed that could be putting Stephenie in an uncomfortable position.

Almost from the moment *Twilight* had gone into production, Stephenie had, on many occasions, been seemingly forced to go on her Web site or do interviews to assure fans that certain choices being made in the films were okay and would not distort their feelings about the characters and the books.

And a case could be made that the filmmakers were becoming a bit tired of the more fanatic elements of Twilight fandom. *Twilight* had been a somewhat open production and little was done to crack down on curious fans who wandered near the filming sites as long as they did not interfere with a shot. On the set of *New Moon*, the sets were very much closed and security was much tighter. Some of that obviously had to do with the growing celebrity of the film's stars and the need not to have an already tight schedule disrupted by fans swarming around the sets. But some fans took it very personally.

It was the fans who were very much on the mind of producer Wyck Godfey on the set of *New Moon* when he talked to a reporter from HitFix.

"It's important to have Stephenie's approval on things," he declared. "But the fans have made these books their own in a way too. Stephenie will be the first to say that they kind of want what they want. So it's [fans' input] something that is helpful but not imperative."

He further acknowledged the working relationship between the filmmakers and the author.

"Stephenie certainly has her opinions of what she wants and most of the time we are bringing her what we think is the right decision. And she has almost always said, 'Yeah, I agree with you.'"

By July, Summit was continuing to attempt to strike while the iron was hot when it was announced that they were officially about to enter pre-production on *Breaking Dawn*, the final entry in the Twilight series. No director was announced, but a lot of speculation about the final chapter was making its way across the Internet and fan sites.

One blog entry had it that *Breaking Dawn* would be made into three films in an attempt to keep the film juggernaut going. And, in a way, that notion would seem to make sense in that Stephenie herself had often speculated on how difficult it would be to jam the entire *Breaking Dawn* story line into ninety minutes. Another topic was the fact that the filmmakers might have to play fast and loose with the sex and birth sequences of the novel in order to avoid an R rating.

Midway through the year, Stephenie, always fan-friendly to a fault, made a decision to shut down her MySpace page in the wake of countless messages and friend requests that were impossible to handle. She told her fans on her Web site that she would continue to monitor other Web sites and post any pertinent updates on her site. Stephenie loved her fans, but she needed to eliminate some of the clutter. Some people were upset at the announcement, but most seemed to understand that, even for Stephenie, there were just so many hours in the day.

The ever-increasing encroachment, positive and supportive as it was, had been a growing concern for some time. She was aware that with worldwide popularity also came fan attention and, in a 2008 interview with the *Los Angeles Times*, she bemoaned how things had most certainly changed.

"When it started out, I'd do an event, maybe forty

people would show up and we'd have this big conversation and really get to know each other. I knew who they were and I actually corresponded with a few of them because I could. But then things just got busier and busier and it got overwhelming. These days, at a signing I can barely say hi to people and that's no fun. It feels horrible to me. So that's changed and that's a little sad. It's great to have things be successful but there are sacrifices that come with it."

It had been almost a sure thing that after the good times and joyous reception she had at the 2008 Comic-Con, Stephenie would once again make the trek to San Diego in 2009. But as the countdown began and the announcement of the *New Moon* film presence was reported, Stephenie's name was conspicuously absent. Stephenie would not show up.

No official reason was given for her absence. But the speculation, as expected, ran wild. Some said she was too busy on her latest book. Others who were more conspiracy minded said she was bothered by some of the things Summit had done regarding *New Moon* (director's change, and so on) and did not want to be involved. Those in attendance at the Comic-Con representing *New Moon* tossed off the "Stephenie's busy writing" or "just wanted to spend some quiet time with her family" whenever the question of her absence was broached. And that seemed to satisfy the die-hard fans who were too excited at the tidbits of *New Moon* that were being trotted out at the film's panel to speculate on why Stephenie had not appeared.

Whatever the reason, Stephenie's absence was duly noted . . . and the worldwide fan base awaited her next move.

fourteen

Perchance to Dream

The first cut of *New Moon* was completed in late August 2009. It would be some time before Stephenie got to see it. Which was just as well because, if you believed the rumors and speculation swirling around her, she was hunkered down and writing something.

But baring any surprises, there would not be a new Stephenie Meyer novel of any kind in 2009. Little, Brown and Company had nothing on their schedule besides the *Twilight Companion*, already long ago written by Stephenie, but with only a vague 2009 release date. So what was Stephenie doing during the summer of 2009? And of particular note was the fact that despite a statement at a 2008 bookstore question-and-answer in which she announced that she had a completed outline for a fifth Twilight book, she had now backtracked on that statement and was being vague about future publishing plans.

But her waffling on the future of Twilight should not have been too much of a surprise. It was not done deliberately and appeared to be a quite natural by-product of the fact that into 2009, Stephenie simply did not know what the future would bring. An interview with *The Wall Street Journal* shortly after the release of *Breaking Dawn* certainly indicated that Stephenie was not closing any doors.

"I was satisfied with the end, but I wouldn't say it's completely tied up," she said. "Life doesn't work that way. The characters seem real to me so you really can't say that's the end. Nothing is really final."

How real the characters had become to Stephenie was revealed midway through 2009 when, in an interview with www.moviephone.com the author said that she was once again dreaming.

"I was sleeping in the guest bedroom because my husband had this horrible cold and I had this weird dream about Edward. Edward showed up and told me I had gotten it all wrong and that he couldn't live off animals. I had the sense that he was going to kill me. It was really terrifying and bizarre; different from every other time I had thought about that character."

In that interview, Stephenie jokingly acknowledged that there might be something in that dream she could use in another book.

Adding fuel to the speculative fire of another book

was the story making the rounds that Stephenie's contract with Summit actually called for a fifth movie, which
could mean either the rumored splitting of *Breaking
Dawn* into two films, perhaps an adaptation of *The Host*
or, as conspiracies go, a pretty good theory that Stephenie had secretly completed a publishable version of *Midnight Sun* and had already struck a deal with the film
production company.

Fuel was added to this rumor when actor Bo Bo Stewart told an interviewer that he was already signed to do
a third Twilight film that would, in fact, be the fifth.
Summit was quick to issue a statement indicating the
actor had misspoken and that there were no immediate
plans for a fifth film.

However, Stephenie shortly thereafter, in comments
reported widely on CNN and countless Web sites, essentially flew in the face of Summit's remarks when she
once again stated that she felt a film version of *Breaking
Dawn* should be two movies.

Stephenie was not the only one being bombarded
with questions about a next book. Little, Brown and
Company was hearing from fans looking for their next
Stephenie fix, and booksellers, keenly aware of the impact her books had on their bottom line, on a constant
basis. All of which led Megan Tingley, Stephenie's editor
at Little, Brown to make a statement to *USA Today*.

"When Meyer might publish a new novel isn't

known," she said. "She's enjoying the writing process without a deadline or targeted publication date."

It was a vague response to be sure and one that many took to mean that Stephenie had suddenly come down with a case of writer's block. Stephenie had often been asked about a problem with that malady. She had often indicated that sometimes she would have difficulty matching up transitional passages between sections of the book but, in the same breath, indicated that there were always ideas and that she had never been in a position of not having something to write about.

The fifth film and fifth book rumors did serve the purpose of fanning the publicity flames for the upcoming *New Moon* movie and nobody was complaining about that. Nor were they too upset when one of those inevitable leaks turned up in St. Louis.

As reported by www.accesshollywood.com on May 11, 2009 a St. Louis beauty salon owner named Casey Ray discovered a copy of the *New Moon* script in a nearby hotel trash bin. Although the hotel was being used by actors filming in the area, nobody could determine how the script found its way out of studio control and into the trash bin. Rather than exploit the find for possible profit, Ray, with the help of a local attorney, returned the script to Summit Entertainment . . . reportedly unread. Summit responded by inviting Ray to the premiere of the movie and thanked her for doing the right thing.

Stephenie, for her part, had pretty much gone underground by the time the trash can flap exploded. Fans continued to burn up the Web sites with speculation of what magic she was most certainly creating at her computer. Stephenie finally came forward toward the end of summer with an update of how she had spent her summer months. And for fans expecting some kind of tremendous announcement, it had to be a bit of a disappointment.

Her Web site blog entry for August 2009 indicated she had been reading a lot of books, listening to a lot of music, and going to the movies.

The books that were high on her recommended list were *Dreamhunter* and *Dreamquake* by Elizabeth Knox and *Catching Fire* by Suzanne Collins. On the music front, Stephenie had been listening to *Merriweather Post Pavillion* by Animal Collective, *Swoon* by Silversun Pickups, *It's Frightening* by White Rabbits, *Horehound* by The Dead Weather, *Veckatimest* by Grizzly Bear, and *Broadcast* by Meese.

It would be understandable that with a big round of media obligations tied in to the November 2009 release of *New Moon*, she would take some time off and do nothing. The consensus was that Stephenie could not just sit around for very long without hitting the computer and writing something.

Since there was so little real news coming from Stephenie's camp at that point, this extremely minor "what I did on my summer vacation" item became a momentary major bit of news. Web sites were playing up the fact that Stephenie was so cool when it came to music and books and some of the more terminally hip outlets were openly amazed that Stephenie could be so current.

Almost lost in the rush to have Stephenie be the arbiter of what people should be listening to and reading were a couple of quite considerable awards that came her way in the early months of 2009. The first was the dual honor of Author of the Year and Teen Choice Book of the Year (for *Breaking Dawn*) awarded by the Children's Choice Awards. Next up was Stephenie making the prestigious *Forbes* magazine list of top one hundred celebrities at number twenty-six.

But with so little hard news to report, it became "silly season" on the many Stephenie Meyer–Twilight Web sites with fans floating all kinds of outrageous rumors and blatant fabrications for their own amusement. One story that got quite a bit of play was that Stephenie Meyer was actually J. K. Rowling. There were also the inevitable rumors that Stephenie was dating despite the fact that everybody on the planet knew that her marriage to Christiaan was rock solid. Mix in the too-many-to-chronicle rumors about Rob Pattinson and it was all good for a laugh to while away the summer until some real news appeared.

Around this time, sources in Forks revealed that Stephenie had rented a house on the outskirts of town (reportedly in the nearby town of Squim), and that she and her family had secretly been taking mini-vacations to the area. During these trips to the area Stephenie apparently took great pains not to be seen out and about and so the occasional report of a Stephenie sighting may actually have had a basis in fact.

There had also been rumors about this time that Stephenie had actually purchased a home in Port Townsend, but nothing that proved out as fact.

Until September 18, 2009, when the *Peninsula Daily News* broke the story that Stephenie and her family had been secretly living part of each year for the past two years in the nearby town of Marrowstone Island.

The news was revealed when the area's Jefferson County Public Utility District updated its water service assessment records. This revealed that Stephenie and her family had purchased a farmhouse on 5.25 acres of land in the tiny community just east of Port Townsend.

Neighbors indicated after the story broke that the family had primarily been in the home during the summer months, had kept a low profile and that security guards had been hired to protect their privacy. Financial and real estate records indicated that the home had been purchased in 2007 for $1.33 million.

Stephenie had been lucky up to this point in that, unlike other authors, she has never had a problem with censorship and particularly bookstores who refused to stock her books. If any store had a problem with the subject matter, they were willing to overlook it in the face of the books flying out of their stores.

But that issue finally did come up in May 2009 when the *Deseret News* reported that Desert Books in Utah had reportedly banned Stephenie's books from the store. Given that Desert Books was owned by the Latter-day Saints and that the store's main focus was on books that reflected Mormon values, it was speculated that the reason for the book's withdrawal was the idea of romance with vampires as presented by Stephenie. Before the controversy could get too far out of hand, a spokesman for the bookstore denied that the books were ever banned and that they had been removed because of "a lack of interest." The spokesperson quickly added that *The Host* remained in the store.

Summit Entertainment continued to bull its way through Stephenie's books with the August 17 announcement that filming had started on *Eclipse* in Vancouver for a projected June 30, 2010, opening. The studio also said that they were proceeding with early pre-production on the movie version of *Breaking Dawn*. And in an almost aside, the studio indicated that *Breaking Dawn* would not be the last movie to be made from a Stephenie Meyer book.

With *The Host* being the only other Meyer book to date, it would appear that is what the studio was talking about. But the rumor mill immediately kicked into high gear that the announcement meant that Stephenie had gotten over her anger over the *Midnight Sun* leak and might have already started working on a complete, more polished version of that book. If that was the case, Stephenie was not saying.

At least until August 11 when a press release from game-maker Wizards of the Coast announced that Stephenie was actually working on something else. Stephenie had agreed to a deal in which she would write *Monster Manual III* for the fourth edition of the company's popular Dungeons & Dragons game. The manual, which is subtitled *Stephenie's Sanctum*, allowed Stephenie to step away from traditional storytelling and to create new takes on different monsters for the game. The book would be available in September. Stephenie was excited at the prospect of creatively stretching her wings.

"The most joyful time writing the Twilight series was when I transformed the vampire and werewolf mythos into something exciting and new," she enthused in a press release. "I can't wait to do the same thing with dragons, trolls, and purple worms."

Stephenie was also taking a stab at creating toys. When Mattel struck a deal for Twilight dolls, which would hit toy shelves in early November 2009, Stephenie wanted to be actively involved. She would end up going to Mattel headquarters and overseeing the art direction of the dolls. During this process Stephenie was adamant about the dolls having the spirit of the characters as she had envisioned them when writing the books.

Stephenie also remained busy on the charity front. Earlier in the year, Stephenie auctioned off signed manuscripts and advance reading copies to help Faith Hockhalter, a long time friend and local bookstore owner, to defray medical bills resulting from a bout with cancer. And she teamed up with a skateboard company to market merchandise from *The Host* whose proceeds would benefit numerous homeless organizations.

Also in late August, it was announced that the comic book biography of Stephenie would soon be available and, in an interesting bit of loyalty to the town where it all takes place, limited edition copies of the book would only be available for purchase or order through the Twilight-only retail store in Forks, Dazzled By Twilight. Like just about everything else Twilight-related in 2009, the comic was slated to come out within shouting distance of the release of the *New Moon* movie.

Although a relatively minor bit of tie-in merchandising, the comic book biography made note of the fact that while the project met wholeheartedly with Stephenie's approval, she did not have any input. So the big fan question of the moment was how their favorite author would be portrayed. As a caped superhero? A very real creature of the night? The company would only hint that Stephenie would be the protagonist of the book. Ryan Burton, the writer of the comic, indicated on the Twilight Treasury Web site that ardent fans had nothing to fear.

"I promise we're being respectful in how we tell the story," he said. "We're making sure the comic touches on little things the fans might know. While presenting the story in a different light."

Into the fall, Stephenie was constantly being apprised of the progress of the movie and was beginning to gear up for the endless publicity interviews she was happy to do to help publicize the film. The questions she fielded this time around were different but, in a sense, also the same.

Reporters fired off the inevitable questions about how she felt about the worldwide popularity of her books, her feelings about going from a humble housewife and mother to famous author. These were the questions she had heard a million times and was fairly rote in firing off the answers. People wanted to know what she was working on currently and she would drop vague notions of future projects but nothing definite.

As it usually happened, questions would be asked about whether the Twilight saga was truly over or whether Stephenie would go back and do it again. A 2007 interview with www.twilighters.org pretty much summed up the author's attitude about going back to the vampire well.

"If I did a book five or six, it would be with different characters, maybe bringing some of the lesser characters to the forefront and telling their stories. But, at this point, I think most of the stories have already been told."

Questions about the film dug a bit deeper. She was peppered with questions about not doing the cameo and how much input she was really having with the films. She was diplomatic in answering those and insisted the relationship between herself and Summit Entertainment was good.

But while outwardly putting out the good word on *New Moon*, it was a safe bet that Stephenie was more than a bit anxious to see the finished product. After all, she had weathered an unexpected change in directors, Summit's tendency to want to replace actors, and the second film's massive, by comparison to *Twilight*, special effects.

It was reported on a Twilight fan site in mid-August that Stephenie had actually seen *New Moon* in a private screening in Phoenix, Arizona, and was reportedly thrilled with what she saw on screen. Whether the report was true or not, it did not have any news life beyond that one report and went quickly off the radar.

During August, it became evident that the plagiarism claims asserted by unknown author Jordan Scott against Stephenie for allegedly taking ideas from her little-known novel *The Nocturne* and incorporating them into *Breaking Dawn* were not going to go away anytime soon. After a cease and desist letter to Stephenie and her publisher failed to get her satisfaction, Scott, aided by lawyer Craig Williams, filed a copyright infringement lawsuit. Scott continued to claim that she wrote her novel at age fifteen and subsequently put it out on her Web site a chapter at a time and that Stephenie had appropriated much of *Breaking Dawn* from her work.

Williams, speaking for Scott, stated in an interview with MTV, "We've laid out the complaints and what the similarities between the two books are. We've detailed more than a dozen plot line and development similarities."

The day after the lawsuit was filed, Jordan Scott was tracked down by MTV, who insisted that she was not challenging the validity of Stephenie's work for publicity purposes.

"It looks like she used my book [*The Nocturne*] as a model," she said. "I don't know if she read a chapter and then wrote a chapter but the similarities are there. I would hope that I could get recognition for my work and an admission from her. I'm not out for money."

Stephenie continued to stay above the situation and

left any response to her publisher, who responded to the latest lawsuit by saying, "The lawsuit was completely without merit and the action is simply a publicity stunt to further Ms. Scott's career."

Stephenie's agent and publisher assured her that these kinds of things happen all the time and were comfortable with having the publisher's lawyers deal with it. But Stephenie did concede that these kinds of things were kind of sad and she continued to insist that all the ideas for her books had come from her and nowhere else.

By mid-August *New Moon* mania had officially begun. Bookstores all across the country had shelves upon shelves packed to the breaking point of hardcover, paperback, and all manner of *Twilight* spin-off books and some tie-in items like shirts. A sign of the influence Stephenie and her creation was having on the entire industry was evident on adjoining display tables where several young adult books, most with vampire or fantastic elements to them, were also piled many copies deep. And if you looked closely, many had been published in the wake of the success of Stephenie's books. For Twilight fans, it was definitely an early Christmas.

Summit also announced during this period that they had entered into an agreement with a professional convention organization called Creation Entertainment to do a series of licensed Twilight conventions all across the country and into 2010. The conventions would feature panels by actors and those involved with the movies, memorabilia dealers, and autograph sessions.

At the first of those conventions, *Twilight* director Catherine Hardwicke told a crowd at one of the panels some of the realities of making that first film. "I loved in the book where Stephenie would describe some of the dreams and so I really wanted to film some of those sequences," she said, as reported by www.mtv.com. "But we had no money. The studio said, 'We can't afford it.' We had to do a lot of things with very little money."

Easily the biggest secret of the moment was what music and which bands would be on the official *New Moon* soundtrack, which ended up being released in early October. Bands like Muse and Radiohead were considered strong contenders, but into August and early September, songs and bands were still being considered. Stephenie was in the midst of suggesting songs for the album and her knowledge and appreciation for new music were integral in the final choices.

What certainly touched Stephenie on a very profound level was the announcement in August that her impact on book buyers had stretched beyond her own titles to revitalize the popularity of a literary classic. Stephenie had always made a point of telling anyone who would listen that she had been reading the classics since childhood and she always remarked that *Wuthering Heights* by Emily Brontë, first published in 1847, was one of her favorites. So much so that she made reference to the novel in her own books and, particularly, during a poignant bit of soliloquy in *Eclipse*. Well, readers in the United Kingdom, thanks to Stephenie, had now discovered *Wuthering Heights* and were buying copies at a rate that catapulted the classic to the top of the U.K. literary charts.

That good cheer was, sadly, counterbalanced by the September announcement of a dubious footnote to Stephenie's popularity. As reported on both www.freak bits.com and www.scifiwire.com, Stephenie's books had captured the title of the most downloaded for free novels of 2009. According to the reports, her books had been downloaded between 100,000 and 250,000 times during the calendar year. Stephenie did not give this report much thought, but it is no surprise that Little, Brown and Company was less than thrilled with this considerable dent in its profit margin.

Into early September, Stephenie was well into promotion mode for the film. She eventually said that she had seen a rough cut of *New Moon* in early fall and was captivated by what the filmmakers had done. Stephenie once again proved herself the master of happy talk. She praised the director, the actors, the studio, and everything connected to the film.

Truth be known, this was the side of Stephenie that could be very pragmatic and businesslike beneath the quiet Mormon exterior. Whether she cared to admit it or not, her blessing carried a massive amount of weight to *New Moon*'s potential audience. To be sure, word of mouth would most certainly bring in a certain amount of people who had not been Twilight fanatics from the beginning.

But what would ultimately put *New Moon* into the box office black was the hard-core fans who would, most likely, go back and see the movie several times in theaters, buy the DVD when it eventually came out, and snap up every bit of merchandising connected to the film. So it only made sense to fuel the fans' expectations, and, in many cases, obsession, that all was right with the world.

The rest of the year passed in a blur. Stephenie was dividing her time between family and promotion but was, with Thanksgiving and Christmas on the horizon, spending as much time as possible at home.

On September 23, the long-running speculation that *The Host* would make its way to the silver screen became a reality when *Variety* announced that the filmmaking team of Steve Schwartz, Paula Mae Schwartz, and Nick Wechster had optioned the non-vampire, science fiction novel for a movie. At Stephenie's suggestion, screenwriter Andrew Niccol (*Gattaca* and *The Terminal*) was selected to write and direct the film.

As with the previous film, Stephenie was most likely

anxious again as the days counted down to the *New Moon* premiere. She had discovered with *Twilight* that she truly enjoyed being part of the glitz and glamour of a Hollywood premiere. And so as she decided what to wear to the premiere and contemplated the walk down the red carpet and the photographer's flashbulbs going off, it was all exciting again.

Stephenie could hardly wait.

It was all a joyous mirror image of what had happened with *Twilight*. The screaming fans going wild as the actors walked, smiling, down the red carpet into the theater. Her stops along the way as reporters thrust out microphones to gauge her anticipation of the film that would unspool on the big screen in front of her in a matter of minutes. And through it all was that smile.

That joyous Stephenie Meyer smile that pretty much told it all.

New Moon's success was validated a few days later on every possible front. That the movie had equaled or surpassed existing box office records was a given. As expected, the critics were split in their assessment of the film, but they tended to come down more on the upside when it came to the relative merits of the movie. It would be a wonderful Christmas present for Stephenie and her family.

To validate the point that a year could not pass without a new book by Stephenie, Little, Brown and Company finally unwrapped the long-in-the-wings *The Twilight Saga: The Official Guide* as a December 2009 gift for her fans.

The Twilight Saga: The Official Guide joined an enormous amount of merchandise and tie-in items that literally glutted the holiday shopping scene, beginning very early in August, and peaking in the November and December run-up to the end of the year. Like every other pop culture mania, big business had jumped to cash in in a very big and overbearing way.

It only took one look at the department store shelves, at everything from the authorized to the knockoffs, to figure out that most of these items would still be on the shelves post-Christmas with a 50 percent or more discount. But, for the time being, it would be safe to say that if the retail economy turned around this year, Stephenie Meyer should have received a large measure of credit.

Because, quite literally, she was everywhere.

As she prepared for the holidays and looked to the future, it appeared that 2010 would be a crossroads of sorts for Stephenie. There would most certainly be other books in the years to come, but as this book goes to press there has been no official announcement. Financially, Stephenie and her family were long since secure for life. All of which brings up the inevitable question.

What's next for Stephenie Meyer? And how does she

move beyond being on top? It is a safe bet that no matter what Stephenie writes from this point on, comparisons will be made and the ghosts of Edward and Bella will always be perched over her shoulder as her family sleeps and she opens other imaginative doors into the night.

Stephenie looked to the future in an interview with *CBS Sunday Morning* that brought her life and career full circle.

"Being where I'm at right now does not make me afraid. In a sense, I guess you have to be afraid and I'm not. I was in a good place before all of this happened. I have this great family and I live in a place that I love. My life was not bad to begin with. It was already good.

"So if everything goes away tomorrow, I'm going to be okay with that."

fifteen

The Town That Stephenie Built

Forks, Washington. B.T. Before Twilight.

As was the case with many towns, Forks was founded by the Quileute tribe of Indians who cleared a good portion of the area to form a natural game preserve for deer, elk, and other animals.

The Quileute tribe made a token appearance in Stephenie Meyer's first book, *Twilight*; most important, the Quileute tribe member, Jacob Black, who was given a werewolf persona by Stephenie. In the second book, *New Moon*, the Jacob Black character and the Quileute tribe were more prominent.

These days, the Quileute tribe has made it plain that Stephenie's account of the tribe and Jacob Black's backstory were purely fictional. But the history of the Quileute tribe is rife with stories with a definite supernatural side to them.

A brief history of the Quileute tribe in the book *Twilight Territory* tells the story of a legendary being called K'wa'iti (also known as the Trickster, the Transformer, and the Changer) who, according to legend, created the first Quileute people from wolves walking on what is today known as First Beach. Stories have also been handed down about a spiritual connection between wolves and orcas (killer whales). There is also the story of what is called "The Boogey Man" that has long been told to Quileute tribe children to get them to obey.

But nowhere in the history of the Quileute is there mention of any spirit resembling a vampire. That was all Stephenie's doing.

While Stephenie did effectively incorporate much of Quileute lore into her books, with no vampire legend to base her story on she invented a vampire tribe called the Cold Ones.

In explaining the background of writing *Twilight* and *New Moon*, Stephenie enlightened readers on her blog of how the Quileute tribe's legends and stories figured into her creative journey.

"The Quileute legends Jacob tells Bella in chapter six of *Twilight* are all genuine Quileute stories that I learned when I was researching the tribe," she explained. "I latched on to the werewolf legend because it fit my sketchy knowledge of vampires and werewolves always being at each other's throats."

The town of Forks was settled in the 1870s. Originally named Fords in honor of one of the earliest settlers, Civil War veteran Luther Ford. History notes that when it was discovered that another town already carried that name, it was renamed Forks in honor of the forks in the Bogacheil, Sol Duc, and Calawah rivers.

In those pioneering days, Forks was primarily a farming community. Around the turn of the century, the townspeople recognized a truly natural resource growing all around them in the form of cedar, elk, spruce, and hemlock, and turned to logging. Farming soon became a secondary occupation and the strength of an ever-growing logging industry literally turned the sleepy little town of Forks into a boomtown.

Things went along just fine until the advent of ecology and environmental advocacy brought Forks to a standstill. Protests surrounding what was perceived as the overcutting of the forest became common. Loggers, once considered a symbol of the independent wild frontier days, were now being tarred as the destroyers of the environment. The death knell came with the controversy over destroying the habitat of one of the local residents, the spotted owl.

"The spotted owl issue resulted in a lot of the federal land being shut down to logging," recalled Chris Cook, editor of the local newspaper, *The Forks Forum*, and author of the regional guide to the area and all things

Twilight, *Twilight Territory*. "That devastated the logging industry and the town's economy has been devastated ever since."

What Forks had going for it at that point was a town that got a lot of rain, was fairly remote (the nearest town of any consequence being Port Angeles some fifty-five miles away), and if the moon hit the surrounding wooded area in just the right way, the area could look a bit spooky. Not the kind of things that the chamber of commerce likes to use as a lure to bring tourists in.

But it was for those very reasons that Stephenie Meyer picked Forks out of an Internet hat as the location for her series of vampire romance novels that began with *Twilight*. For Stephenie, Forks had it all.

Early on in her research, Stephenie had considered setting her first book, *Twilight*, in Arizona. But seeing as how Arizona was known more for its heat and that Stephenie was writing the novel in the midst of an Arizona summer that topped out at 115 degrees, it made perfect sense to use colder, wetter, and more supernatural-appearing climes. She turned her search to Google and punched in the question of the wettest place in the United States. Forks came up with big capital letters.

Cook reported that, through July 2009, an estimated 16,000 visitors a month have descended on the sleepy town of 3,500. And the economy? Well, conservative estimates, by way of the chamber of commerce, have the city income increasing by 300 percent over the past three years. And one need only look at Forks's main drag to figure the reason why.

From the Forks Outfitters to the Chinook Pharmacy and all the stores in between, it's all Twilight all the time. Dazzled By Twilight, a Twilight-only store, carries all the latest tie-in merchandise. Sully's Drive-In features the Bella Burger on its menu. It's the rare store that does not have something Twilight to tempt fans—some from as far away as Denmark and Armenia—who consistently make the pilgrimage to their holy grail, the birthplace of their favorite books and their favorite lovers, Edward and Bella. Hotels are constantly booked up to the point where some local residents have taken to renting out rooms in their houses. Guided tours of Forks's landmarks leave several times a day.

And it is the lure of tourist dollars that is showing signs of spreading to other small towns in the Pacific Northwest. Nearby Port Angeles recently held a two-day Twilight-themed event and has done its best, albeit on a smaller scale, to bring in the Twilight fans.

"The fans don't see our town as normal," chuckled Cook in explaining what Stephenie Meyer has brought to the town. "The way I see it, what the town is experiencing is kind of like *The Truman Show*. We don't know if we're on the outside or the inside. It's like the day-today life goes on. But, at the same time, there's like this whole other reality happening."

It is this "whole other reality" that has been a constant source of amusement and amazement for Cook who, as the author of *Twilight Territory*, has become a local celebrity as well as the unofficial spokesman for those seeking insights into Forks and its ties to the biggest-selling author on the planet.

A writer recently rang up Cook to ask questions about the area for an upcoming book that would speculate that cults were growing up around the obsession with the Twilight books. When a local sign proclaiming a Twilight sentiment was burned during the night, Cook and a couple of well-placed calls turned this minor piece of vandalism into a story in a major Washington daily paper. And the Internet being what it is, he had a good laugh when the story began making the rounds of Twilight-oriented Web sites.

Cook recalled hearing word of mouth about this author Stephenie Meyer who had chosen Forks as the location for her novels around 2005. And that was only after Stephenie, in 2004, made a trip to Forks, a stopover that had made little impact on the people of Forks.

"When she first came here, nobody had any specific questions for her because nobody was really knowledgeable about her or her book," remembered Cook.

"We knew that she was wandering around the real estate and visitors industry Web sites and visiting the national parks and looking at all kinds of maps and surveys. We assumed she was doing some research for background on her book."

For their part, the Quileute tribe took a watch-and-wait attitude about this unknown novelist who was reportedly incorporating local tribal lore in her first book. Their main concern was that Stephenie not use the Quileute hook as a mere jumping-off point for her own flights of fancy. The Quileutes, like almost all Native American tribes, have been alternately patient and impatient with having to clarify their history and legends to people. They could only hope that Stephenie would get it right.

When *Twilight* came out, it was an instant sensation just about everywhere, except, laughed Cook, in Forks.

"That first book really didn't impact anything here. The nearest bookstore to Forks is in Port Angeles, which is more than fifty miles away. The grocery store and the pharmacy only have small book sections. When the first book came out, it didn't even make the library."

Forks's library manager Theresa Tetreau eventually ordered a copy and, in the spring of 2006 was astonished to receive a phone call from Stephenie about coming to Forks to do a small community book signing.

The library, members of the chamber of commerce, and others quickly formed a committee and came up with the idea of a book signing and reading to take place in Forks on July 20, 2006.

Chamber of commerce executive director Marcia Bingham recalled in an interview for the book *Twilight Territory* that Stephenie's 2006 visit was an unexpected success. "She was charming, very happy to be here, and very pleased with the look of Forks. There were about 125 people gathered in Tillicum Park and they had come from Canada, California, Washington, and Oregon. I thought this was big but I did not have an inkling that the book would become a national bestseller."

Cook said that nobody thought too much of the event at first. But that was until the first trickle of outsiders came to town.

"It was pretty strange when we saw some fans from outside Forks show up for the book signing. Forks is out in the sticks and kind of at the bottom of the totem pole when it comes to bigger cities in the state. So to actually have people coming out here for a story about Forks was highly unusual."

Stephenie's visit to Forks was a success, but nobody imagined it would do anything else for the town. But Forks's pulse spiked again in the spring of 2007. First there were dozens of fans showing up to see the town and the real-life landmarks they had only read about in

Stephenie's books. People of Forks started seeing flecks of gold at the end of the Twilight rainbow—especially when dozens became hundreds.

"The city started doing some small things in 2007," said Cook. "We printed up vampire hunting permits and people had to go around to different stores in town to get stamps on their permit. There were a couple of places that were selling Twilight-related items, but it wasn't a major deal. One of the stores was selling Twilight hoodies and beanies and another was selling T-shirts. But it wasn't much at that point.

"But we began to notice some things. People weren't just coming here from nearby towns. They were coming from California, Utah, and other states. And we started seeing signs on their cars that said 'Team Edward' and 'Team Jacob' and 'Forks or Bust.' At first it was like 'what's that?' Then we started understanding the whole thing."

By the time 2008 rolled around and *Breaking Dawn*, the final book in the series, was about to be published, the town of Forks began to understand and acted accordingly. Marcia Bingham of the chamber of commerce and Mike Gurling of the visitor's center put their heads together in an attempt to come up with ways to capitalize on the growing interest in the town. A combination Stephenie Meyer Day and Bella's Birthday event was created for September 13. Store owners were encouraged to stock Twilight-themed items. A special map emphasizing the locations that appeared in the books was created.

"The town did a special midnight event for the official release of *Breaking Dawn*," related Cook. "We made a stamp that said 'Made in Forks' that we stamped on the books bought at our stores. People began putting up signs in front of their houses saying that this was the home of such and such a character from the books. It even got to the point where people were taking sand from the beach, putting it in vials, and selling it as Forks sand. But the local Indian tribe who owns the land got upset about that and made them stop."

While the Quileutes were adamant about keeping the sanctity of their culture, they also saw the possibility of the tourist dollar and soon Twilight-themed merchandise began appearing in the windows of motels and gift shops on their land.

Despite location-scouting expeditions by Summit Entertainment, neither of the movies made of *Twilight* or *New Moon* were shot in Forks. Cook offered that while some of the local town promoters were disappointed that the movie company did not set up shop in Forks, for most of the residents it was like water off a duck's back.

"I actually believe that it helped the town that the

movies were not shot here," he explained. "People have read these books a lot of times and they can come here and there's this real-life world they only know from the books they can wander around in. Stephenie Meyer's books are not like the Harry Potter books. The places she mentions are real and people can come here and see them."

Cook acknowledged that the increase in the tourist trade has caused occasional traffic problems along the main drag. "But we haven't had the crime or theft. Gangs haven't come through here. Initially some goths were showing up, but they decided that the whole Twilight thing wasn't dark enough or cool enough for them so they stopped coming around. It's mostly families. It's become like a beach town. They show up at ten in the morning and they're gone by six. There's been virtually no problems between the tourists and the locals."

Cook laughingly related that the townspeople don't think too much beyond the fact that there's money coming into the town.

"But the neat thing is that once people find out you're from Forks, you tend to become an instant celebrity. The principal of the high school was at an airport recently and he had a Forks varsity jacket on. Some kid came up to him and asked if he was from Forks. He said yes and the kid started screaming. Before he knew it, the principal had a mob of kids surrounding him. There have also been guys going online, claiming to be from Forks, so they could pick up girls. But some of the local kids got wind of that and ratted them out."

Evidence of just how long a ride it could be for Forks came with the recent announcement that a documentary on the town, entitled *Twilight in Forks: The Saga of the Real Town*, had been filmed with almost no fanfare and was released on DVD in October 2009. The documentary, by producer and onetime Forks resident York Bauer and director Jason Brown, looks at the real-life town and the impact the popularity of Twilight has had on it.

Given the notoriety the town has received, it comes as a surprise that the local residents are less than enthusiastic about the source material. Cook claimed that there are not many hard-core fans in Forks proper and that only about one person in twenty has actually read the books. He is also quick to point out that there is almost no interest in the author's latest book, *The Host*. With the last book in the Twilight series out and no immediate plans for a follow-up in the works, one has to ultimately wonder how long the interest in Forks will remain. Cook said he sees no end to it.

"With the new movie coming out, it's sparked a whole new wave of people coming out here. Originally we saw the reader types. Now we're getting the people who first saw the movie and are now reading the books. This is going to go on for a long time to come."

And nobody was more aware of the continued interest in all things Twilight than the Quileute tribe who, in June 2009, announced that they had retained the services of a professional public relations firm to handle any media inquiries about the tribe.

"It was important for us to partner with a native-based organization that we feel identifies and respects our core values," said tribal chairwoman Carol Hatch. "We want to make welcome people from all around the world seeking information about our people and our land."

There have been some minor adjustments in Forks to accommodate tourist traffic. The WELCOME TO FORKS sign, often a first stop photo opportunity for visitors, has had its location readjusted to avoid street congestion. And in lieu of the thousands of people who showed up in Forks for the annual Bella's Birthday and Stephenie Meyer Day in September, the city's police department implemented a police bike patrol to help control the pedestrian traffic in and around Forks's main drag.

The weather forecast for the weekend celebration was for cloudy and rainy. For any other celebration that would have spelled disaster. But the chamber of commerce was quick to remind anyone who asked that this was a Twilight celebration and that's what the fans expected. If it had been sunny, they would have been disappointed.

And like every new situation, there have been some naysayers. A rumor among many of the locals in the area is that the goth community is moving into the area and attempting to settle in as a permanent colony. And occasionally there will be compaints about the traffic. But, for the most part, the good people of Forks and the Twilight universe have learned to coexist.

Part of the continued allure of Forks may well settle on the recent report that Stephenie and her family have moved to the area to live. One real estate agent has claimed that he has sold a house to Stephenie in nearby Port Townsend. And Cook is more than willing to help the story along by reporting several Stephenie Meyer sightings unreported to the press.

"She was supposedly spotted eating in a restaurant in nearby Port Angeles and she has been reported several times recently in Forks. All the stores have these guest books for people to sign and one lady showed me her guest book and said Stephenie and her friends had come there. I looked at the signature.

"And the signature sure looked real to me."

bibliography

Twilight. Publication date: October 5, 2005

New Moon. Publication date: September 6, 2006

Prom Nights from Hell (story in anthology). Publication date: April 2007

Eclipse. Publication date: August 7, 2007

The Host. Publication date: May 6, 2008

Breaking Dawn. Publication date: August 2, 2008

Monster Manual III: Stephenie's Sanctum. Publication date: September 2009

The Twilight Saga: The Official Guide. Publication date: December 2009

filmography

Twilight. Release date: November 21, 2008

New Moon. Release date: November 20, 2009

Eclipse. Release date: June 30, 2010

Breaking Dawn. Release date (tentative): 2011

directing

"Resolution" by Jack's Mannequin (music video)

miscellaneous writing

"Hero at the Grocery Store" (short story). *The Ensign,*
    December 2006

"Resolution" by Jack's Mannequin (video treatment)

the music in her mind

It goes without saying that music has been a guiding force in the inspiration and emotion that populates the novels of Stephenie Meyer. Her tastes in music are constantly changing. But these are the bands and performers that were there from the beginning.

twilight

Travis, My Chemical Romance, Radiohead, Coldplay, Linkin Park, OMD, David Gray, Dido, Muse, The Cranberries, Collective Soul, Billy Joel.

new moon

The Flaming Lips, Linkin Park, Muse, All-American Rejects, Marjorie Fair, Matchbox Twenty, Jimmy Eat World,

The Vines, Coldplay, Rooney, The Fray, Evanescence, Brand New, Relient K, The Verve Pipe, Fatboy Slim, Foo Fighters, Sugarcult, Armor for Sleep, Blue October.

eclipse
Elbow, Keane, Coldplay, Muse, All-American Rejects, Blue October, The Killers, The Magic Numbers, Dashboard Confessional, Alanis Morissette, Placebo, Brand New, Travis, OK Go, My Chemical Romance, Patrick Wolf, Arcade Fire.

breaking dawn
The Beach Boys, Billy Idol, INXS, Muse, Blue October, Plain White T's, Jack's Mannequin, Coldplay, Fuel, Nine Inch Nails, Aerosmith, Incubus, Interpol, Korn, TV on the Radio, My Chemical Romance, Motion City Soundtrack, R.E.M., Jimmy Gnecco, The Smashing Pumpkins, Right Said Fred, Jimmy Eat World, Linkin Park, 3 Doors Down, Simon and Garfunkel, Death Cab for Cutie, Muse, OK Go, Travis, Arcade Fire.

midnight sun
Matchbook Romance, Placebo, Three Days Grace, Kaiser Chiefs, Linkin Park, Gomez, Editors, Bush, Blue October, Muse, Taking Back Sunday, Anberlin, Fuel.

the host

Death Cab for Cutie, Linkin Park, Muse, Eisley, Foo Fighters, Nine Inch Nails, Editors, Sting, My Chemical Romance, Placebo, Travis, The Killers, Three Days Grace, Phoenix, Rob Dickinson, Arcade Fire, Jack's Mannequin, U2, All-American Rejects.

sources

An undertaking of this kind is only as good as its sources of information and, in the case of *Stephenie Meyer, The Unauthorized Biography of the Creator of the Twilight Saga,* I was fortunate to have access to the work of a number of professional journalists who knew how to poke, prod, and get to the heart of the matter.

In particular I would like to personally thank Professor Steven Walker of Brigham Young University who shared with me his firsthand impressions of Stephenie Meyer in her college days. I would also like to extend warm wishes to Chris Cook, editor of the *Forks Forum,* the newspaper of record in Forks, Washington, and the author of the guidebook *Twilight Territory: A Fan's Guide to Forks and LaPush,* for his insights, anecdotes, and some photos of Stephenie's early visit to the town that have not been seen before. And finally I would like to thank Linda Ellinwood for beating the streets of Port Angeles in search of journalistic gold.

Many magazines, newspapers, and other news sources made writing this book a joy. They include *Arizona Republic*; Associated Press; *Chicago Tribune*; *The Courier-Mail*; *Daily Herald*; *Daily News*; *Deseret News*; *Entertainment Weekly*; *Forks Forum*; *The Guardian*; *Kansas City Star*; *Kirkus Reviews*; *The Los Angeles Times*; *Media-Blvd*; *National Post*; *The New York Times*; *Paris Match*; *Phoenix New Times*; *Pittsburgh Post-Gazette*; *The Post and Courier*; *Publishers Weekly*; *Rolling Stone*; *School Library Journal*; *Seattle Post-Intelligencer*; *Time*; United Press International; *USA Today*; *Variety*; *Vogue*; *VOYA*; and *The Wall Street Journal*.

The advent of the Internet and the wide array of Web sites helped flesh out the story. They include www.about.com; www.accesshollywood.com; www.aceshowbiz.com; www.allthingsgirl.com; www.amazon.com; www.bbspot.com; www.bloody-disgusting.com; www.bookreporter.com; www.bookstories.com; www.canmag.com; www.collider.com; www.cullenboysanonymous.com; www.digestive.niddk.nih.gov; www.efluxmedia.com; www.entertainment.times.online.com; www.entertainmentweekly.com; www.eonline.com; www.examiner.com; www.firststep.me.com; www.freakbits.com; www.hitfix.com; www.indiaforums.com; www.

motleyvision.com; www.moviephone.com; www.mtv. com; www.newmoonmovie.org; www.people.com; www. quileutelegend.com; www.rte.ie.com; www.scifiwire. com; www.sheknows.com; www.stepheniemeyer.com; www.stepheniesays.livejournal.com; www.timesonline. com; www.twilightlexicon.com; www.twilightmoms. com; www.twilighttreasury.com; www.tmz.com; www. yadultbooks.central.com; and www.wikipedia.com.

And finally several off-the-beaten-track sources that provided important pieces to the puzzle. These include *Breaking Dawn* concert tour question-and-answer transcripts for New York, Pasadena, and Chicago; *CBS Sunday Morning*; Reelz Channel; Summit Entertainment press releases; *Today*; Wizards of the Coast press release; and *World News Tonight*.

The
twilight
Companion

The unofficial guide to the
bestselling twilight series.

Completely
updated

Lois H. Gresh

The Twilight series by Stephenie Meyer
follows an unlikely couple: Bella, a gawky
teenage girl stuck in a new town, and
Edward, a gorgeous vampire who has
sworn off human blood. Added to the mix
is Jacob Black, a werewolf who also loves
Bella. Seductive and compelling, the
four-book series has become a worldwide
phenomenon.

EVERMORE

THE IMMORTALS

Alyson Noël

SOMETIMES LOVE IS ETERNAL.
FOR GOOD . . . FOR EVIL . . .
FOREVER

Sixteen-year-old Ever Bloom is the sole survivor of a car accident that killed her family. Exiled to sunny California, Ever is haunted by her little sister and by the ability to see people's auras, hear their thoughts and know their entire life story by touching them. She wants to hide from the world, but when a stunningly handsome new guy arrives at school, she can't seem to keep away. Falling in love with Damen is dangerous – he's not what he seems. But if Damen is her destiny, how can Ever walk away?

A selected list of titles available from Macmillan Children's Books

The prices shown below are correct at the time of going to press. However, Macmillan Publishers reserves the right to show new retail prices on covers, which may differ from those previously advertised.

Lois H. Gresh

| The Twilight Companion | 978-0-330-51089-9 | £6.99 |

Alyson Noël

| The Immortals: Evermore | 978-0-330-51285-5 | £6.99 |
| The Immortals: Blue Moon | 978-0-330-51286-2 | £6.99 |

Elizabeth Chandler

| Kissed by an Angel | 978-0-330-51149-0 | £6.99 |

Poems chosen by Gaby Morgan

| In My Sky at Twilight | 978-0-230-74586-5 | £6.99 |

All Pan Macmillan titles can be ordered from our website, www.panmacmillan.com, or from your local bookshop and are also available by post from:

Bookpost, PO Box 29, Douglas, Isle of Man IM99 1BQ

Credit cards accepted. For details:
Telephone: 01624 677237
Fax: 01624 670923
Email: bookshop@enterprise.net
www.bookpost.co.uk

Free postage and packing in the United Kingdom